I'm A Christian

Now What?

TODD CAPPS
CONTRIBUTING EDITOR

ALISON CREEL   BILL EMEOTT

RANDY FIELDS   AMY GRUBB

VICKI HULSEY   CINDY LEACH

JON MERRYMAN   JERRY VOGEL

LifeWay Press®
Nashville, TN 37234

ISBN: 9781415873236
Item #005490151
This book is a resource in the
category of the Christian Growth Study Plan Course.
Dewey: 242.62
SUBHD: CHILDREN—DEVOTIONAL LITERATURE \ CHRISTIAN LIFE \ REGENERATION (CHRISTIANITY)

Printed in the United States of America.

Kids Ministry Publishing
LifeWay Church Resources
One LifeWay Plaza
Nashville, Tennessee 37234-0172

We believe the Bible has God for its author; salvation for its end;
and truth, without any mixture of error, for its matter
and that all Scripture is totally true and trustworthy.
To review LifeWay's doctrinal guideline
Please visit www.lifeway.com/doctrinalguideline.

TABLE OF CONTENTS

HOW TO USE YOUR
I'M A CHRISTIAN, NOW WHAT? JOURNAL

Asking Jesus to be your Savior and Lord is the most important decision you will ever make. No one can take that decision away from you. Now that you are a Christian, it is important to learn more about being a Christian. That's the purpose of this journal. The information on these pages will help you learn how to live in ways that please and honor God. Here are some helps on how to use your journal.

√ Ask your parents to read page 5 with you. After reading the promises, you and your parents should sign the pledges.

√ Begin with the introduction to the first set of devotions (page 6). This information and set of devotions will help you understand what a quiet time is and why you should study your Bible. Only complete one day's activities at a time.

√ Locate the "Verse of the Day" passage in your Bible. Take a few minutes to read and think about the verse(s).

√ Challenge yourself to read additional verses by locating, reading, and thinking about the "Challenge" verses.

√ Make notes, write, and draw in your journal. This is *your* journal, so take notes about what you learn and how God speaks to you.

√ Listen for God to speak to you each day.

√ Keep your journal in a safe place.

√ Start again (where you stopped) if you miss a day.

√ Ask your parents (or another adult) to help you if you do not understand something.

√ Follow the prayer suggestions on each devotion. Take time to listen to what God says to you.

√ Take as long as you need each day to complete the activities.

√ Pay attention to what you read. As you work through your journal, you may think you already read some of the information in a previous study. You are CORRECT! Some of the information about living the Christian life relates to more than one area and is included more than one time.

Included in your journal are some pages your parents should read. When you discover these pages, take your journal to your parents and ask them to read the information.

PARENT/CHILD COMMITMENT

Dear Parents,

Your child has made the most important decision he will ever make. His decision to ask Jesus to be his Savior and Lord is one that not only affects his life now, but for eternity. God instructs you, parents, to teach your child (Deuteronomy 6:4-9). This *I'm a Christian, Now What?* journal is designed to help your child grow in his knowledge and understanding of the Christian life. Each week, your child will explore a new topic and have six daily devotions to complete. If possible, begin on Monday with the introduction and Day 1 devotion. No devotions are included for Sundays, so use this as a time to worship (see p. 68) with your child.

Encourage your child to complete as much of the journal individually as possible. Allow him to learn how to use his Bible, respond to questions, and pray. Be available and ready to help when he needs assistance. One of the most important things you can do is pray for your child on a daily basis.

Ready to get started? Read the pledges below with your child. Take a few minutes to pray together, then sign the pledges.

PARENT AND CHILD PLEDGES

PARENT'S PLEDGE

✓ I promise to pray for and encourage you each day.
✓ I promise to help you when you need help.
✓ I promise not to read your journal unless you give me permission.

Signed _____

Date _11/24/14_____

CHILD'S PLEDGE

✓ I promise to pray for myself each day.
✓ I promise to ask for help when I need help.
✓ I promise to make it a priority to complete my devotion each day.

Signed _Kayelym_____

Date _November24 2014_____

WHAT IS A QUIET TIME?
WHY SHOULD I STUDY MY BIBLE?

VICKI HULSEY

Who is your best friend? What do you and your best friend enjoy doing together? How much do you know about your best friend? Do you know what her favorite food is? What about her favorite book, TV show, color, or hobby? How do you know these things? You know because you spend time with your friend. Now that you are a Christian, you have a special relationship (friendship) with God. God wants to spend time with you. He wants you to know who He is and learn as much as you can about Him. Spending time with God is called a quiet time—a time when you read, study your Bible, and pray (talk to and listen to God).

Think about the answers to these questions: Do you ever wonder how a person can be God's friend? Can a person talk to God? Can God hear when someone speaks to Him? Can someone know what God is like? Can someone know what He wants her to do? The answer to these questions is YES! The good news is, each of these questions apply to you! When you study your Bible, you get to know more about God and grow in your relationship with Him. How does knowing God wants you to know who He is make you feel?

God has a plan for how you can grow in your friendship with Him. Learning about God through the Bible and prayer are the best ways to get to know God. Here are some things to think about.

- **God loves you.** He wants to have a relationship with you. He knows everything about you and He wants you to know everything about Him, too.
- **God wants to spend time with you EVERY DAY.** The Bible is God's message, His words to YOU. God will speak to you as you read the Bible. The Bible helps you learn about God and His plans for your life.
- **The Bible helps you know how to please God.** The Bible shows Jesus' life as the example for you to follow. Jesus completely, 100%, obeyed God. Now that you're a Christian, it is important for you to follow Jesus' example. You can learn to make good choices by studying Jesus' life as written about in your Bible.
- **Prayer is another great way to grow in your friendship with God.** God wants you to talk with Him like a good friend, but He also wants you to listen to Him. You can tell God what you are thinking, how you are feeling, and what you need. God will hear your prayers.

Christians need to find time each day to read the Bible and pray. Some Christians call this their **quiet time.** When you are quiet and listen to God, you will be able to hear and understand what God is saying to you. Ready to get started? This week's devotions (quiet times) will help you understand more about having a quiet time.

DAY 1 — A QUIET PLACE

VERSE OF THE DAY: Matthew 6:6
CHALLENGE: Matthew 6:5-8

DO! Complete the "Where Can I Have My Quiet Time?" activities on pages 10-11.

STOP what you are doing. Find a quiet place to talk to God. Tell God what you are thinking and feeling.

LISTEN to God as He speaks to you. Think about the words of Matthew 6:6. Ask God to help you hear Him.

LOOK around you. What can you thank God for today? Draw a picture of the items.

✓ God is everywhere at all times.
✓ God wants you to communicate with Him through praying and reading the Bible.
✓ God hears and answers prayers.
✓ God will speak to you through the Bible.

PRAY Thank God for wanting to have a relationship with You. Ask Him to help you make it a priority to spend time with Him each day.

DAY 2 — THREE QUIET TIME Ps

VERSE OF THE DAY: Psalm 1:2
CHALLENGE: Psalm 1

DO! Complete the dot to dot. What letter did you discover? How many Ps can you find? Let the letter P help you remember three things about your quiet time.

PRIORITY is something that is very important. Is having a quiet time important to you? _yes_ A quiet time helps you grow in your relationship with God.

PREPARATION is getting ready for something. Here's some help on getting ready.
→ Set an alarm to remind you.
→ Place your Bible, pencil, and journal in the same place so you can find it every day.
→ Open your Bible to tomorrow's verses after finishing today's study.

PLAN what you will do. Practice now!
→ Begin with a simple prayer such as, "God, help me learn about You today."
→ Read the day's verses.
→ Write down what God is teaching you.
→ Pray, asking God to help you apply what you learned to your life.

✓ The Bible is true.
✓ The Bible is God's message.
✓ The Bible tells what Jesus is like.
✓ The Bible helps you understand how God wants you to live.

PRAY Ask God to help you follow the 3 Ps and grow in your relationship with Him.

DAY 3

HOW DOES THE BIBLE HELP?

VERSE OF THE DAY: Psalm 119:34 / CHALLENGE: Psalm 119:33-40

 Follow these clues to discover a type of book.

R P H K P U W M O F
D I C T I O D A R Y

→ Change the Ps to Is.
→ Change the R to a D.
→ Change the H to a C.
→ Change the M to an A.
→ Change the F to a Y.

→ Change the W to a N.
→ Change the O to a R.
→ Change the K to a T.
→ Change the U to an O.

What type of book did you discover? _DICTIODARY_

A dictionary helps you understand words you do not know. Think about how these books help you:
→ Math book
→ Social Studies book
→ Language book
→ Music book
→ Bible

✓ The Bible helps you know what is right and wrong.
✓ The Bible helps you know God's commandments.
✓ The Bible tells you how to live the Christian life.
✓ The Bible tells you what God wants you to do through stories about people and events.
✓ The Bible helps you learn from the mistakes of others.

PRAY Thank God for giving you the Bible to help you know what is right and wrong.

DAY 4

TAKE IT WITH YOU!

VERSE OF THE DAY: Psalm 119:11 / CHALLENGE: Psalm 119:9-16

 Think of all of the places you will go today. In the backpack, draw the items you need to take with you.

Think about what you would take if you were going to these places:
→ Swimming pool
→ A friend's house for a sleepover
→ On vacation

Would you take your Bible with you?

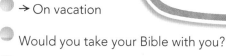

✓ You can take your Bible with you everywhere you go.
✓ God wants you to remember what you read during your quiet time. When you memorize Bible verses, the Bible will be with you wherever you go.

Finish this sentence after reading today's verse (Psalm 119:11).

I can memorize Bible verses to help me not __SIN__ against God.

PRAY Ask God to help you remember what you read in the Bible.

DAY 5

THE BIBLE HELPS YOU GROW!

VERSE OF THE DAY: 2 Timothy 3:16
CHALLENGE: 2 Timothy 3:10-17

 DO! Complete the chart.

	AS A BABY	NOW
My weight	6lb 7h	49.6
My height	19 in	48 in
My hair color	very browo	brity blonde
My favorite food	formula	salad

Find a picture of you as a baby. What are some ways you have grown? What are some things that helped you to grow?

helps me felle beter

Just like your body is growing and changing, you also need to grow as a Christian. What are some ways the Bible can help you grow?

my hair got barker I'vg nown

KNOW!

√ You grow in your relationship with God by studying your Bible, praying, and worshiping and obeying Him.

√ You grow in your relationship with God by spending time with other Christians.

√ You may not understand everything you read in the Bible. As you grow in your relationship with God, pray for understanding, and He will let you know what the verses mean.

PRAY Ask God to help you understand the Bible so you can grow as a Christian.

DAY 6

DON'T GIVE UP!

VERSE OF THE DAY: Jeremiah 33:3
CHALLENGE: Joshua 1:1-9

DO! How would your best friend feel if you did not talk to her for several days? Do you think she would wonder if you were mad at her?

Ask your parents if you can call a family member you have not talked to in several weeks. After the call, think about these questions: *How did the person respond? Was she excited to hear from you? What did you talk about? What did you learn from your family member?*

How do you think God feels when you go several days or weeks without spending time with Him?

bad

KNOW!

√ God wants you to spend time with Him EVERY DAY.

√ God will forgive you when you do not spend time with Him.

√ You can spend time with God anywhere and at anytime. He is always ready to listen to you.

√ The more you develop the habit of having a quiet time, the easier it is to continue.

PRAY Ask God to help you not to give up if you miss your quiet time. Thank Him that you can talk to Him and read your Bible anytime and anywhere.

WHERE CAN I HAVE MY QUIET TIME?

Use the code box to discover 10 places you can have your quiet time.

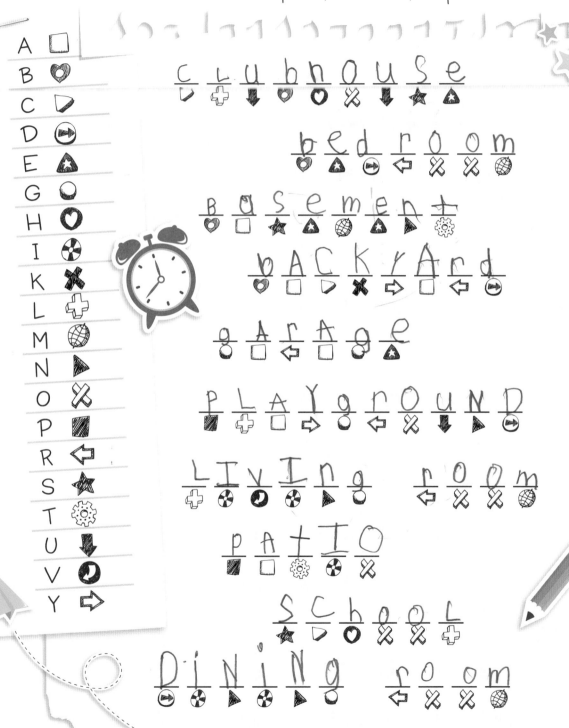

clubhouse

bedroom

Basement

bACKyArd

gArAge

PLAYground

LIVIng room

pATIO

School

DINIng room

WHERE IS THE BEST PLACE FOR ME TO HAVE MY QUIET TIME?

THINK ABOUT THESE THINGS AS YOU DECIDE:

? Is the place quiet so I can focus on what I am learning?

Yes

? Is the place private enough so I can read, write, and listen to God without someone interrupting me?

Yes

? Is the place somewhere I can go to every day?

yes

? Would any of the places I discovered in the puzzle (page 10) be good for my quiet time?

yes

My quiet time place will be ___my room.___

I will have my quiet time at ___6:00 at night___

HOW DO I KNOW THE BIBLE IS TRUE?

JERRY VOGEL

The Bible is the most amazing book ever written. The Bible tells you everything you need to know about God's love and His magnificent plan for your life. Many claims are made within the Bible that help prove it to not only be the most wonderful book ever written, but also the most important book in the world.

The Bible teaches you ...
- God's story of Himself.
- the details of the creation of the universe.
- the story of how people are God's most special creation.
- God's laws people are to follow.
- how people rebelled (turned away from, disobeyed) against God.
- the work God did through Jesus to provide salvation.
- what it means to be part of God's "forever family."
- how you should live in relationship to God and people.
- what happens after physical death.
- the purpose and meaning of life.

How do you know if the teachings of the Bible are true? As you study the Bible, you will discover information to help you know everything in the Bible is TRUE.
- The Bible itself makes the claim to be true (Psalm 119:160; 2 Timothy 3:16).
- Jesus taught that Scripture is true and important (Matthew 4:1-11).
- The Bible is historically correct. The names of many of the Roman officials in the Bible have been confirmed (proven to be correct) by ancient historical records and archeology (a science that deals with past human life and activities).
- Bible prophecies continue to come true. Jesus Himself fulfilled prophecies made several hundred years before He was born (Isaiah 7:14; 9:6).
- The Bible has been taken care of and passed down through the generations of time. The Bible is very old, and has not changed through thousands of years. What was true when God told people what to write in the Bible is still true today.
- The whole Bible points to Jesus Christ as the Savior of the world and continues to change lives.

Each of the devotionals that follow will help you better understand important characteristics of the Bible. These are characteristics the Bible teaches about itself. God and the Holy Spirit will help you understand these truths as you spend time reading and studying each day. When you read the Bible, you are actually connecting with God and what He wants to say to you.

DAY 1

THE BIBLE IS GOD'S WORD

VERSES OF THE DAY: 2 Timothy 3:16-17 / CHALLENGE: Nehemiah 8:1-12

DO! Use the code box to discover five ways people communicate with one another.

	1	2	3	4	5
A	A	F	I	N	S
B	C	G	L	O	T
C	E	H	M	P	X

t e l e p h o n e
B5 C1 B3 C1 C4 C2 B4 A4 C1

t e x t m e s s a g i n g
B5 C1 C5 B5 C3 C1 A5 A5 A1 B2 A3 A4 B2

f a c e t o f a c e
A2 A1 B1 C1 B5 B4 A2 A1 B1 C1

m a i l n o t e s
C3 A1 A3 B3 / A4 B4 B5 C1 A5

e m a i l
C1 C3 A1 A3 B3

What other ways do people communicate?
Circle the ways you communicate with people.

KNOW!

✓ God communicates in a variety of ways (prayer, people, thoughts, and the Bible).
✓ God inspired (told people) what to write in the Bible.
✓ The Bible is God's message about Himself.
✓ The Bible is the ONLY written word of God.

PRAY Thank God for the Bible. Ask Him to help you better understand the things you read.

DAY 2

THE BIBLE WILL NEVER GO AWAY

VERSE OF THE DAY: Isaiah 40:8 / CHALLENGE: 1 Peter 1:25

DO! Circle the things that will last forever.

? Did you circle the Bible? All of the other items will one day disappear.

? How long is forever? How many years?
  ∗ Forever is FOREVER! (People have a hard time understanding forever.)
? What about the Bible (not the "book" you own … but the words found in the Bible)? God's words will last forever.

KNOW! The teachings in the Bible will last forever.

PRAY Thank God for the Bible. Praise Him for giving you His words that will last forever.

DAY 3
THE BIBLE IS A TRUE BOOK

VERSE OF THE DAY: Psalm 119:160
CHALLENGE: John 8:31-32

 List three things you know are true. List three things you know are false.

TRUE	FALSE
_____	_____
_____	_____
_____	_____

Was the Bible on the *True* list?

KNOW!

✓ Many scientific truths are recorded as facts in the Bible such as the shape of the world as it hangs in space. Job 26:7 and Isaiah 40:22 make remarkable statements contrary to the ancient belief that the earth was flat, or square.

✓ Ecclesiastes 1:7 tells how water from a stream returns to its source. Perhaps without even understanding it, the writer of Ecclesiastes recorded the process of evaporation, condensation, and precipitation long before scientists figured it out.
✓ The stories in the Bible are REAL and TRUE.

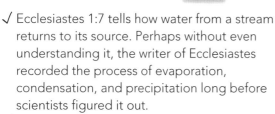

PRAY Thank God for the Bible. Tell Him about your favorite Bible story. Thank Him for what the story teaches you.

DAY 4
THE BIBLE IS ALIVE

VERSE OF THE DAY: Hebrews 4:12
CHALLENGE: Matthew 4:4

 How would you describe something that is alive? Draw pictures of six things in your house that are alive.

How do you know these things are alive? What do you think it means to say "the Bible is alive?"

KNOW!

✓ To say "the Bible is alive" means that it continues to speak to people today. When you read the Bible, you can learn how to make choices, treat other people, and live in ways that please and honor God. The Bible helps you know what to do!
✓ The Bible is for EVERYONE—all peoples of the world. The Bible speaks to people in all languages and in every country of the world.
✓ The Bible has been translated into hundreds of different languages. Some people still do not have the Bible in a language they can read and understand.

PRAY Thank God for the Bible. Tell God one thing the Bible has taught you that you need to change. Ask for God's help in making this change.

THE BIBLE CHALLENGES PEOPLE TO RESPOND TO GOD

DAY 5

VERSES OF THE DAY: Proverbs 3:5-6 / CHALLENGE: 1 Peter 5:7

DO! Throughout Scripture, God challenges people to be and do certain things. Locate these three verses in your Bible. Read and match the verses to the correct statements.

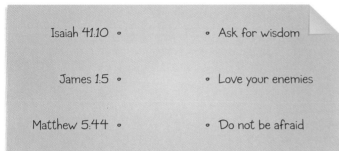

Isaiah 41:10 •   • Ask for wisdom

James 1:5 •   • Love your enemies

Matthew 5:44 •   • Do not be afraid

Can you do these things this week? How? When? Where? Think of other things the Bible challenges you to do. Are you willing to do what God says?

KNOW!

✓ The Bible says that salvation through Jesus is a gift and that EVERYONE can choose to accept God's gift.
✓ The Bible tells people how to obey God (it also tells about people who disobeyed God and what happened to them).
✓ The Bible tells how people's lives were affected by their responses to God.

PRAY Ask God to help you always respond in ways that please and honor Him.

THE BIBLE HELPS GUIDE PEOPLE'S LIVES

DAY 6

VERSE OF THE DAY: Psalm 119:105 / CHALLENGE: John 8:12

DO! Complete the drawing of the lighthouse. What purpose does a lighthouse serve?
   The Bible is like God's lighthouse. The Bible helps guide and keep you safe. What are some areas in your life where you need guidance? _____
Look at the list below. Do you need help with these areas? If the area you need help in is not listed, write on the blanks.

KNOW!

✓ The Bible helps me understand how God wants me to live.
✓ The Bible helps me make decisions.
✓ The Bible tells me how to love and serve God as well as how to treat other people.

PRAY Ask God to help you follow the teachings in the Bible.

☐ Obeying my parents
☐ Treating my brothers/sisters with respect
☐ Spending time completing my
   I'm a Christian, Now What? journal

☐ Telling my friends about God
☐ Sharing my toys
☐ _____
☐ _____

FUN BIBLE FACTS

It's time to discover some fun stuff about the Bible.
Share these facts with your family and friends.

The Old Testament was written in Hebrew (HE broo) and Aramic (ar uh MAY ihk). The New Testament was written in Greek.

Methuselah (mih THOOZ uh luh) was the oldest man in the Bible. He lived to be 969 years old.

The shortest verse in the Bible is John 11:35.

The longest chapter in the Bible is Psalm 119.

The word Christian only appears three times in the Bible (Acts 11:26; 26:28; 1 Peter 4:16).

The word Bible does not appear in the Bible. Bible comes from the Greek word Biblia, meaning "books."

The most frequently named animal in the Bible is the sheep.

The longest name in the Bible is Mahershalalhashbaz (MAY hehr-SHAL al-HASH baz) (Isaiah 8:1).

The Bible contains 1,189 chapters.

The Bible contains more than 3,200 questions.

Ruth (ROOTH) and Esther (ESS tuhr) are the only books in the Bible named for women.

The tallest man in the Bible was Goliath (guh LIGH uhth). He was 9 feet 9 inches tall.

The shortest chapter in the Bible is Psalm 117.

The average reader can read the whole Bible in about 70 hours.

The books of the Bible did not have chapter or verse numbers when they were written.

Dogs are mentioned in the Bible, but cats are not.

Two men, Enoch (EE nuhk) and Elijah (ih LIGH juh) never died. God took them to heaven.

A donkey actually talked (Numbers 22:28-30).

In the King James Version of the Bible, Ezra (EZ ruh) 7:21 contains all of the letters of the English alphabet except one. The letter "J" is not used.

John 3:16 is one of the most memorized verses in the Bible.

The only nuts mentioned in the Bible are almonds and pistachios.

David is the most mentioned man's name in the Bible (approximately 1,118 times depending on Bible translation).

The longest verse in the Bible is Esther 8:9. Count the words.

HOW DO I STUDY MY BIBLE?

TODD CAPPS

Beginning to study your Bible may be difficult at first. You may wonder "Where do I begin?," "How much do I read every day?," or "How do I remember all the stuff I read?" Here are some ways you can study your Bible.

Study **verse-by-verse**. Begin with the first verse of a Bible book, and read 10-12 verses a day. Look up words you do not know and keep notes in a journal of things you learn. Think about these questions as you read the verses:

◎ What did God want the people to know?
◎ What does God want me to know?
◎ How can I apply these verses to my life?

A second way to study is to learn about **people in the Bible.** What do you know about Noah, Esther, Daniel, Rahab (RAY hab), or the Beroeans (bih REE uhns)? Did you know the Bereoans searched the Scriptures to make sure what Paul taught is true? (Acts 17:10-15)

As you begin a person study, pick a person such as Ruth, Mary Magdalene (MAG duh leen), Caleb, or Titus (TIGH tuhs). These individuals are important, but there is not so much information that you will become confused learning about them. When you have a better understanding of how to study Bible people, then you can study Moses, King David, Peter, or Paul.

Think about these questions as you study a Bible person:

◎ Who is the person?
◎ What did the person do?
◎ What can I learn from the person?

A third way to study your Bible is to study **words or concepts** such as prayer, peace, love, forgiveness, or even animals in the Bible. Select a word and find verses in the Bible that contain the word. A Bible concordance (a book listing all of the Bible words in alphabetical order) will help you.

Think about these questions as you study:

◎ How is the word used?
◎ What does the word mean in the verses?
◎ What does the word mean to my life?

The more you read and study the Bible, the easier it will become to understand and apply to your life. Ask your parents if it is OK for you to underline or highlight verses in your Bible. You may also want to make notes about what you learn as you study.

A VERSE-BY-VERSE STUDY OF THE BOOK OF MARK, PART 1

VERSES OF THE DAY: Mark 1:1-8 / CHALLENGE: Isaiah 40:3

DO! Imagine God told you to write a book about Jesus. What would you write in your book? What would you name the book? Draw a picture of the cover of your book.

Based on Mark 1:1-8, what does God want people to know?

KNOW!

✓ The Book of Mark was written by a Jew named Mark.

✓ Mark was a cousin of Barnabas (BAHR nuh buhs) and went with him and Paul on the first missionary journey.

✓ Mark talks about Jesus as the ultimate servant.

✓ Mark uses the word *immediately* over 40 times.

_____

_____

God wants me to know _____ .

I can apply these verses to my life by _____ .

PRAY Ask God to help you learn about Jesus' ministry as you study the Book of Mark.

A VERSE-BY-VERSE STUDY OF THE BOOK OF MARK, PART 2

VERSES OF THE DAY: Mark 1:9-13 / CHALLENGE: Matthew 3:13–4:11

DO! How would you answer these questions about Mark 1:9-13?

? What did God want the people to know?

? What does God want **me** to know?

? How can I apply these verses to my life?

   Draw a picture of what you think Jesus' baptism looked like. Draw a picture of your baptism. What is the same in the pictures? What is different?

JESUS' BAPTISM   MY BAPTISM

KNOW!

✓ The Jordan River is the longest and most important river in Palestine (PAL uhs tighn).

✓ In the Bible, a dove is a symbol of peace and innocence. A dove is first mentioned in Genesis 8:8-12.

✓ A *wilderness* is "an area of land with little rainfall and few people."

✓ To *tempt* someone is "to try to get a person to make a wrong choice or take action that is wrong."

PRAY Make a list of the things you are tempted to do. Ask God to help you not give in to the temptations.

DAY 3

STUDY THE WORD "OBEY"

VERSE OF THE DAY: Ephesians 6:1
CHALLENGE: Exodus 20:1-17

DO! Circle the people and things you obey.

 Parents

 Bible

 Teachers

 Directions on your homework

 Traffic Laws

 Police

 Friends

 Doctors

Why do you obey these people and things?

_____

What would happen if you did not obey them?

_____

✓ *Obey* means "to hear God's Word and act on it."
✓ In the Old Testament *obey* means "to hear."
✓ In the New Testament *obey* means "to hear," "to listen," and "to trust."
✓ When a person hears or reads God's Word, he needs to obey what he hears or reads. To really hear God's Word is to obey God's Word.

How many times is the word *obey* in the Bible? If your Bible has a concordance in it, look up the word *obey*. Locate and read some of these verses. What do these verses tell you to do?

PRAY Ask God to help you *obey* Him every day.

DAY 4

STUDY ANIMALS OF THE BIBLE

VERSES OF THE DAY: Genesis 1:24-25
CHALLENGE: Genesis 1

DO! Can you think of the names of animals that begin with each letter of the alphabet? Write or draw them beside the letters.

A   B   C   D

E   F   G   H

I   J   K   L

M   N   O   P

Q   R   S   T

U   V   W   X

Y   Z

KNOW! The Bible tells about many different animals. Read about these in your Bible.
✓ Bear: 1 Samuel 17:34-35
✓ Cattle: Psalm 50:10
✓ Frog(s): Exodus 8:1-15
✓ Horse(s): 1 Kings 4:26
✓ Lion: Daniel 6:16
✓ Serpent: Psalm 58:4
✓ Sheep: 1 Samuel 17:34

PRAY Thank God for the animals He created.

DAY 5 — LEARNING ABOUT A BIBLE PERSON: JOHN THE BAPTIST, PART 1

VERSES OF THE DAY: Matthew 3 / CHALLENGE: Luke 1

DO! When you hear the name John the Baptist, what comes to mind? Answer these questions about John.

What did John teach? (Matthew 3:2-3)

What did John wear and eat? (Matthew 3:4)

How did people respond to John? (Matthew 3:5-6)

Who did John preach about? (Matthew 3:11-12)

What did John do to Jesus? (Matthew 3:13-17)

Draw a picture of John the Baptist.

KNOW!

✓ John the Baptist was related to Jesus (Luke 1:18-25,36,39-45,57-80).
✓ John's father, Zechariah (ZEK uh RIGH uh) was a priest (Luke 1:5).
✓ Because Zechariah did not believe he would have a son, he was unable to speak until after John's birth (Luke 1:8-20,57-80).
✓ John's birth was announced by the angel Gabriel (Luke 1:11-20).

PRAY "God, help me have the courage to tell people about Jesus like John the Baptist did."

DAY 6 — LEARNING ABOUT A BIBLE PERSON: JOHN THE BAPTIST, PART 2

VERSES OF THE DAY: Mark 6:14-29 / CHALLENGE: Matthew 3:12-16

DO! Think about the things you learned about John the Baptist in yesterday's study. Answer these questions about John.

How did John die? (Mark 6:16-29) _____

_____

What did John tell King Herod? (Mark 6:18) _____

_____

_____

KNOW!

✓ Many Bible people gave their lives to follow Jesus.
✓ John the Baptist believed Jesus is God's Son.
✓ John told people things they did that did not please God.
✓ John was killed because he obeyed God.

PRAY Some people today are killed because they obey God. Write a prayer for people who obey God even when their lives are in danger.

THE BOOKS OF THE OLD TESTAMENT

The Old Testament consists of 39 different books.
The books are separated into 5 divisions.

THE BOOKS OF LAW
(All 5 were written by Moses)

GENESIS (JEN ih siss) is about the beginning of things, including how God created the world and everything in it, the great flood, the Tower of Babel, and the beginnings of the nation of Israel.

LEVITICUS (lih VIT ih kuhs) continues the history told in the Book of Exodus. The book also contains the ceremonial and religious law.

EXODUS (EK suh duhs) tells about the people of Israel leaving (exodus) Egypt, how they wandered in the wilderness, and how God gave His law to the people of Israel.

DEUTERONOMY (DOO tuh RAHN uh mih) contains a second telling of the giving of the Law. The book ends with Moses' death.

NUMBERS (NUHM buhrz) tells of the census or numbering of the people of Israel and the history of their journey after leaving Egypt.

JUDGES (JUH jihz) tells about the leaders God gave the Israelites after Joshua died and what those leaders did.

RUTH (ROOTH) contains the story of God's care for Naomi and her daughter-in-law, Ruth. The book also tells how Ruth met and married Boaz and had a son named Obed.

1 AND 2 SAMUEL (SAM yoo el) are named for the prophet Samuel. The two books tell about the first two kings of Israel: Saul and David.

JOSHUA (JAHSH yoo uh) tells how the Israelites entered and became the owners of the land God promised them.

1 AND 2 KINGS (KINGZ) continue the history of Israel from King Solomon through the division of Israel into two kingdoms, Israel and Judah, and into the exile of both kingdoms. These books cover a period of about 425 years.

1 AND 2 CHRONICLES (KRAHN ih kuhls) are the records of the history of Israel and Judah.

OLD TESTAMENT HISTORY

EZRA (EZ ruh) begins with the return from the exile. The book covers a period of about 80 years, telling of the rebuilding of the Jerusalem temple and how the Jews decided to obey God again.

ESTHER (ESS tuhr) tells how Esther became queen and how she prevented the killing of the Jews.

NEHEMIAH (NEE huh MIGH uh) continues the Jews' history with the return from exile and how God used Nehemiah to rebuild Jerusalem's city wall.

POETRY

JOB (JOHB) is the story of a man named Job, whom God tested.

PSALMS (SAHLMZ) is a collection of one hundred fifty "songs" written by different authors over a long period of time. King David wrote many of the Psalms.

PROVERBS (PRAHV uhrbs) contains godly wisdom that helps people to live in ways that please God, gives practical advice, and makes wise observations.

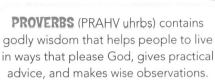

ISAIAH (igh [eye] ZAY uh) includes prophecy about the coming of the Messiah.

ECCLESIASTES (ih KLEE zih ASST eez) is another book of wisdom written by Solomon.

MAJOR PROPHETS

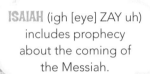

JEREMIAH (JER ih MIGH uh) calls the people of Judah to turn away from their idol worship and other sins.

THE SONG OF SONGS (SAHNG-ahv SAHNGS) is a love poem that King Solomon wrote.

LAMENTATIONS (LA men TAY shuhnz) is a lament, or a song of mourning, over the sins of Judah. Jeremiah wrote this book.

EZEKIEL (ih ZEE kih uhl) tells of God's judgment on Israel and other nations, but also predicts the future blessings of God and salvation of His people.

DANIEL (DAN yuhl) speaks of the power of God over people of all nations.

Read about the Books of the New Testament on pages 98-99.

MICAH (M<u>I</u>GH kuh) warns the people of Israel and Judah of coming judgment and offers forgiveness for those who repent.

JONAH (JOH nuh) tells the story of the prophet who did not want to tell Israel's enemies about God's love.

NAHUM (NAY huhm) speaks of God's judgment of Nineveh in order to offer comfort to Judah.

AMOS (AY muhs) called on the people of Israel to stop worshiping idols and to quit being mean to the poor.

OBADIAH (OH buh DIGH uh) teaches God will punish those who trouble His people.

HABAKKUK (huh BAK kuk) speaks of God's power over the nations.

JOEL (JOH el) calls the people to repent and warns them about God's judgement. The book also tells about the coming of the Holy Spirit on all believers.

HOSEA (hoh ZAY uh) xpresses God's love for His sinful people, Israel.

HAGGAI (HAG igh [eye]) calls those who returned to Jerusalem from exile to complete the rebuilding of the temple.

ZEPHANIAH (ZEF uh NIGH uh) foretells the day of punishment and the reward of the good.

MALACHI (MAL uh kigh) contains prophecies about the Messiah and calls the Jews in Jerusalem to turn from their sins and renew their relationship with God.

ZECHARIAH (ZEK uh RIGH uh) tells about the coming of the Messiah and gives hope to the Jews who had returned to Jerusalem from exile.

MINOR PROPHETS

WHAT IS PRAYER? HOW DO I PRAY?

AMY GRUBB

Now that you have a personal relationship with God, He wants you to communicate with Him OFTEN. You talk to God and listen to Him through prayer.

Prayer isn't complicated. You don't have to say special words when you pray. God just wants you to talk with Him. Remember, God loves you and wants to hear about your good times, what troubles you, what you need and want, and what you're thankful for. He also wants you to listen to what He wants to tell you.

You can pray anywhere at any time. You can pray with your eyes open or closed. You can kneel when you pray to show that you honor God, but you can also pray while standing. You can pray while walking your dog or riding your bike—just keep your eyes open! You can pray quietly to yourself or speak the words of your prayer aloud. God will hear your prayer no matter how you pray.

If you aren't sure how to pray, learn from Jesus. He shared a model prayer with His disciples (Matthew 6:9-13). The word *pray* can even help you to remember things to share with God.

Prayer is powerful. The Bible tells many stories of how God hears and answers prayer. God's answers to prayers have freed people from prison, closed the mouths of hungry lions, and caused fire to rain down from heaven. The Bible promises when you pray, God will hear and answer your prayers—but in His own way.

Prayer is also personal. How do you develop a friendship with someone? You have to spend time with that person. As you spend time communicating with God in prayer, He'll become even more real. The more time you spend with God, the better you know Him.

P = PRAISE

R = REPENT

A = ASK FOR OTHERS

Y = YOURSELF

WHAT IS PRAYER?

VERSE OF THE DAY: Psalm 17:6
CHALLENGE: Daniel 6:13-22

 Picture the most powerful person in the world. Now imagine that you receive a phone call from that person. What would you do? Hang up? Put the phone down until you have some free time? Of course not! You'd talk with that person right away!

The most powerful Person in the universe wants to talk with you! God wants you to talk with Him through prayer.

Write the message below on several sticky notes. Place the notes in a place you see every day.

Dear _____,

I'd really like to talk with you today!

Love, God

✓ Prayer means "talking and listening to God."
✓ God wants you to share concerns with Him.
✓ God wants you to pray for other people.
✓ God hears your prayers 24/7 (24 hours a day, 7 days a week).
✓ God will answer your prayer.

PRAY Thank God, the Creator of the universe, for inviting you to talk with Him.

JESUS' PRAYER

VERSES OF THE DAY: Matthew 6:5-8
CHALLENGE: Matthew 6:9-13

 Go into a private room in your house and close the door. Place an empty chair in front of you. Imagine Jesus is sitting in the chair. What kind of things do you want to share with Him? Tell Him what's bothering you, what excites you, what your needs are, and what you are thankful for.

Think about Jesus' prayer. His prayer isn't long or difficult. Jesus praised God, asked for forgiveness for sins, and mentioned the needs of Himself and others.

Rewrite Jesus' prayer using your own words.

✓ God is everywhere at all times. He hears everything you say to Him.
✓ Jesus, God's Son, taught His disciples how to pray.
✓ You can follow the examples, commands, and teachings of Jesus.

PRAY Thank God for sending Jesus to teach you how to pray.

DAY 3

HOW DO I PRAY?

VERSES OF THE DAY: Matthew 6:5-13 / CHALLENGE: 1 Thessalonians 5:16-18

 Read the words on the thumb, palm, and index finger. Repeat the same thing for the other fingers. (OK, the "Y" does not make sense—it will in a minute.) What messages did you discover?

P stands for PRAISE. Praise God for all He has done for you.

R stands for REPENT. *REPENT* means "to turn or change from disobeying God to obeying Him."

A stands for ASK. God wants you to ask Him for the things you and other people need.

Y stands for YOURSELF. God wants you to pray for yourself.

✓ God understands what it means to be human.
✓ God knows you have many cares and concerns.
✓ God wants you to share your cares with Him in prayer.
✓ God not only wants you to talk to Him, He wants you to listen to Him. God will tell you what He wants you to do when you listen.

PRAY Using your hand as a guide, praise God, repent of your sin, and ask Him for things for others and yourself.

DAY 4

PRAYER IS POWERFUL

VERSE OF THE DAY: James 5:16 / CHALLENGE: 1 Kings 18:16-39

DO! If you could design your own superhero, what would he look like? Draw him on the paper. What would make him different from a regular person? What special powers would he have?

Would you like to have the same powers as your superhero? What would you do with your powers? A superhero's powers are imaginary (made up, not real), but the power of prayer is REAL. The Bible says a Christian's prayers have great power.

✓ The Bible tells how people's lives were affected by their responses to God.
✓ The Bible is full of true stories about the power of prayer.
✓ Paul and Silas prayed and were freed from prison (Acts 16:25-34).
✓ Samson prayed for his strength to return (Judges 16:28).
✓ Elijah prayed for a dead boy to be brought back to life and the boy was revived (1 Kings 17:17-23).

PRAY Thank God for giving you the power of prayer. Ask Him to meet your needs and the needs of others according to His will.

DAY 5 — PRAYER IS PERSONAL

VERSES OF THE DAY: Philippians 4:6-7
CHALLENGE: 1 Samuel 1:10-17

DO! Stand in front of your mirror and think about what worries you. School? Sports? Friends? Parents? How do you look when you are worried?

What if you could erase (get rid of) all of your worries? How would you look and feel then?

God's Word says to pray always and to give your cares to Him. He'll take care of them. He loves you!

Hold your book in front of a mirror to discover four important things about prayer.

GOD WILL HEAR YOU WHEN YOU PRAY.

GOD ANSWERS PRAYER WITH YES, NO, OR WAIT.

GOD KNOWS WHAT IS BEST FOR YOU.

GOD IS READY TO LISTEN TO YOU RIGHT NOW.

KNOW!

✓ God is all-powerful. He can handle all your cares and concerns.
✓ God is all-knowing. He knows what you need and want, but He wants you to tell Him about your concerns.
✓ Nothing is too big or small to tell God.
✓ God loves you and wants to develop a close relationship with you through prayer.

PRAY Ask God to help you stop worrying and trust Him more each day.

DAY 6 — PRAYING FOR OTHERS

VERSE OF THE DAY: Ephesians 6:18
CHALLENGE: Ephesians 6:16-20

DO! On the building, write the names of five families who live close to you. What do you know about these families? What are their needs? How can you pray for these families?

Take a few minutes and pray for each family by name. Ask God to meet the needs of each family.

KNOW!

✓ God always hears and answers prayers.
✓ The Bible is full of examples of people praying for others:
  * Moses prayed for the Israelites and God did not punish them (Exodus 32:11-14).
  * Jesus prayed for His followers (John 17:20).
  * The church prayed for Peter and he was freed from prison (Acts 12:5-11).
  * Elijah prayed for Israel and God sent fire from heaven (1 Kings 18:36-39).
  * Prayerwalking is walking and praying at the same time (yes, you keep your eyes open). As you walk around your neighborhood, school, grocery store, or other places, pray for the people you see. Ask God to meet their needs.

PRAY Ask God to bless the families you listed above.

HOW TO KEEP A PRAYER JOURNAL

A prayer journal is a book in which you write down information about your prayer requests. Writing down your prayer requests allows you to see how God has worked and is continuing to work in your life. Check out this page of a prayer journal.

DATE	MY PRAYER REQUEST	HOW GOD ANSWERED	DATE GOD ANSWERED
Monday 3/2	I need help learning to spell the words for my spelling test.		
Tuesday 3/3	Marcia is going to visit her aunt and uncle this weekend.		
Tuesday 3/4	My grandpa's shoulder surgery is tomorrow.	Grandpa did not have any problems with his surgery.	3/5
Wednesday 3/5	Grandpa's shoulder surgery	Grandpa is feeling much better. He should get to go home Saturday.	3/6
Wednesday 3/5	Spelling test tomorrow		

Notice the boxes under "How God Answered" and "Date God Answered" are not filled in for three of the requests. These events have not taken place yet. After the test, these boxes can be filled in to show how God answered the prayer. When Marcia returns, information can be written about her trip.

HERE ARE SOME THINGS YOU CAN DO TO KEEP A PRAYER JOURNAL.

→ Ask your parents to buy you a notebook.

→ Draw and label columns like the ones below.

→ Write or draw pictures to represent your prayer requests. (It's OK to have more than one request each day.)

→ Write or draw how God answered your prayer (after He does so).

→ Fill in the date God answered your prayers.

→ Look back at the ways God answered your prayers.

→ Keep your prayer journal in a special place. (It is OK not to let anyone read your prayer requests.)

REMEMBER

God answers prayers in three ways:

→ **YES**—He will give you what you asked for.

→ **NO**—He will not give you what you asked for.

→ **WAIT**—You will have to wait for Him to answer you.

DATE	MY PRAYER REQUEST	HOW GOD ANSWERED	DATE GOD ANSWERED

God knows what is best for us!

HOW IS MY LIFE DIFFERENT SINCE BECOMING A CHRISTIAN?

BILL EMEOTT

When you became a Christian, your life CHANGED! Did God give you a new body? (*No.*) Did you completely stop sinning? (*No.*) Did you stop enjoying your favorite hobbies, sports, art, or music? (*Probably not.*) So, how is your life different since becoming a Christian?

While the changes in you are not physical and usually do not include a complete overhaul (change) in your God-given personality, you are different and because of that, your life is different.

Read what the Bible says in 2 Corinthians 5:17. The writer of 2 Corinthians was the apostle Paul. He wrote these words to the church at Corinth. Many of the people in the church were new believers in Jesus, just like you. Paul helped them understand four things in this verse:

- Anyone in Christ—This means people who are believers in Jesus, Christians.
- A new creation—You have a new way of seeing things and are controlled by new desires (wants); you want to live in ways that please and honor God.
- Old things are gone—Your behavior has changed. You are no longer controlled by your old sinful ways (that does not mean you will never sin again, we will talk about that later).
- New things have come—You have a new relationship with Jesus with new desires that result in a new behavior.

So, you know that when you became a Christian, some things in your life are different than before. What exactly are these things? Here are a few of the "biggies:"

- You are forgiven of your sins (1 John 1:9).
- You have eternal life with Jesus (John 3:16).
- You choose to let Jesus control your life (John 14:15).
- You want to follow what the Bible teaches and God's plan for your life (Psalm 119:11).
- You seek to know God better by studying your Bible, praying, worshiping, and serving Him (2 Timothy 2:15).
- You want to tell other people what Jesus did for you (2 Timothy 1:8).

Can you think of other ways your life has been different since you became a Christian?

DAY 1

I'M FORGIVEN OF MY SINS

VERSE OF THE DAY: 1 John 1:9
CHALLENGE: Luke 15:11-32

 DO!
→ Make a list (below) of things that come to your mind when you think of your sins.
→ Look over the list.
→ Ask God to forgive you of your sins.
→ Mark through each item.
→ Be glad God forgives you of your sins.

KNOW!
✓ Even as a Christian, you will sometimes choose to disobey God and sin.
✓ God still loves you and will forgive you, but He wants you to try not to sin again.

PRAY Thank God for forgiving your sins. Ask Him to help you learn to obey Him in EVERYTHING!

DAY 2

I HAVE ETERNAL LIFE WITH JESUS

VERSE OF THE DAY: Romans 6:23
CHALLENGE: John 14:1-6

DO! If you could give someone the greatest gift on earth, what would you give him? Draw or describe the gift here.

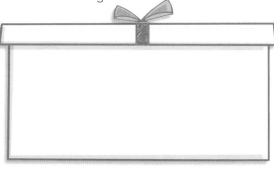

What made you decide to give this gift?
   Complete a chore or task for someone in your home or neighborhood. When the person asks who did the work, you can say, "I did it for you. I gave you a gift."
   Think about how the person felt having you to do the chore.

 KNOW!
✓ God gave you the gift of eternal life.
✓ Jesus died on a cross for your sins, rose from the dead, and is now in heaven. Jesus is preparing a place for you.
✓ When you die, you will go to heaven and spend eternity there. How long is eternity? FOREVER!
✓ Have you ever thought—EVERYONE DIES? The difference is Christians know when they die they will go to heaven and have eternal life with Jesus. People who do not accept Jesus as Savior and Lord will be separated from God FOREVER!

PRAY Thank God for the gift of eternal life He gave you when you became a Christian.

DAY 3

I CHOOSE TO LET JESUS CONTROL MY LIFE

VERSES OF THE DAY: Mark 12:30-31 / CHALLENGE: Mark 12:28-34

DO! Learn the sign language for these words.

Love

Lord   God

Heart

Soul

Mind

Strength

Neighbor

KNOW!

✓ Giving Jesus control is allowing Him to be Lord (or boss) of who you are.
✓ God wants you to live every day in ways that please and honor Him.
✓ You can follow God's plan for your life when you let Him be in control of what you say and do, how you act, and the decisions you make.

PRAY Ask God to guide and control your life.

→ Say the verses using the sign language.
→ Teach the sign language to your friends.

DAY 4

I DESIRE TO FOLLOW THE BIBLE AND GOD'S PLAN FOR MY LIFE

VERSE OF THE DAY: Jeremiah 29:11 / CHALLENGE: Luke 18:18-29

DO! Circle people who help you know what to do.

Pastor

Parent

Police Officer

Teacher

Doctor

When you grow up, what type of work do you want to do? How do you think you will feel if God wants you to do something different? Will you be willing to do it?

KNOW!

✓ God places people in your life to help you know what to do.
✓ God has a plan for your life. You can know and understand His specific plan and trust Him to help you make the right decisions.
✓ God wants people to be transformed (changed) by Him.
✓ The Holy Spirit helps you grow in your relationship with God.

PRAY Thank God for the Bible. Ask God to help you follow His plans for your life.

DAY 5

I WANT TO KNOW GOD BETTER

VERSE OF THE DAY: Matthew 6:33
CHALLENGE: 2 Timothy 3:14-17

 Circle the statements you believe are true.

God is everywhere at all times.

God has power to do anything.

God is real, the one true God.

God hears me when I pray.

God wants me to know Him.

Did you circle all of the statements?
They are all TRUE!
Think about your best friend. What are some things you and your best friend like to do together?

KNOW

✓ Best friends know each other really well. They know each other's likes and dislikes. When you take time to get to know someone, it is easier to understand who she is and what she enjoys doing. That's the same with God. The more you know Him, the more you know what He wants you to do.
✓ Through Bible verses and stories, God helps you know Him. As you read and study the Bible, you learn how He created the world, how He cares for people, and how He sent Jesus to earth. God loved the people in the Bible, and God loves you too.

PRAY
Thank God for His Word. Ask Him to help you learn who He is as you study the Bible. Ask God to speak to you each day.

DAY 6

I WANT TO TELL PEOPLE WHAT JESUS DID FOR ME

VERSES OF THE DAY: Matthew 28:19-20
CHALLENGE: Acts 10

DO! Write a poem about what being a Christian means to you.

List the names of people who need to hear your poem.

KNOW

✓ God wants people around you to know about Him.
✓ God wants you to tell people how He has made a difference in your life.
✓ The Holy Spirit helps believers tell people about Jesus and how they can ask Him to be their Savior and Lord.

PRAY
 Ask God to give you the courage to share your testimony with non-Christians.

THE DISCIPLES OF JESUS

Think about how your life is different since you asked Jesus to be your Savior and Lord.
Jesus chose 12 men to follow Him and be His disciples.
Read the information about these men. On the journal page 37, write what you
hope will be written about you because you followed Jesus.

The Bible tells nothing about JAMES except for his name.

ANDREW was a fisherman with his brother Peter on the Sea of Galilee. Jesus called Andrew to be a disciple while he was fishing (Matthew 4:18-20). Andrew brought his brother Peter to Jesus (John 1:40-42), and told Jesus about the boy with the loaves and fishes (John 6:8-9).

JOHN was a fisherman on the Sea of Galilee with his father, Zebedee (ZEB uh dee), and his brother James. Jesus called John to be a disciple while he was mending (repairing) nets (Matthew 4:21-22). John helped Peter prepare the Passover meal (Luke 22:8). From the cross, Jesus told John to care for His mother (John 19:26-27).

THADDAEUS (THAD ih uhs) asked Jesus how He was going to reveal Himself to the disciples and not to the world (John 14:22).

JAMES was a fisherman on the Sea of Galilee (GAL ih lee) with his father, Zebedee, and his brother John. Jesus called James to be a disciple while he was mending nets (Matthew 4:21-22). James was the first disciple to be killed for his faith (Acts 12:2).

The Bible tells nothing about SIMON except for his name.

BARTHOLOMEW (bahr THAHL uh myoo) or NATHANAEL (nuh THAN ay uhl) was invited to see Jesus by Philip. Jesus called him a "true Israelite" (John 1:45-51).

JUDAS ISCARIOT (JOO duhs-iss KA(a)R ih aht) was keeper of the disciples' money bag. Judas betrayed Jesus for 30 pieces of silver (Matthew 26:15). Judas was sorry for what he had done and hanged himself (Matthew 27:3-5).

Jesus called MATTHEW to be a disciple while he was a tax collector in Capernaum (kuh PUHR nay uhm). Matthew invited Jesus to a dinner where his friends could meet Jesus (Matthew 9:9-13).

SIMON PETER was a fisherman with his brother Andrew on the Sea of Galilee. Jesus called Peter to be a disciple while he was fishing (Matthew 4:18-20). Jesus helped Peter to walk on water (Matthew 14:29). Peter denied Jesus before His crucifixion (Luke 22:54-62) and was later forgiven by Jesus (John 21:15-19).

THOMAS encouraged the disciples to go with Jesus and die with Him (John 11:16). Thomas wanted evidence (proof) that Jesus had risen from the dead (John 20:25). Jesus showed Thomas His hands and side to prove His resurrection (John 20:27).

Jesus called PHILIP to follow Him as a disciple (John 1:43). Philip found Nathanael (nuh THAN ay uhl) and told him about Jesus (John 1:43-45). Philip went with Andrew to bring some Greeks to Jesus (John 12:20-22).

WHAT I HOPE
WILL BE WRITTEN
ABOUT ME
AS A FOLLOWER
OF JESUS.

FIND THE DISCIPLES' NAMES IN THE PUZZLE.

```
J  U  D  A  S  I  S  C  A  R  I  O  T  I
O  Q  W  N  E  R  T  Y  U  I  O  P  H  J
H  B  J  D  V  P  M  N  Q  W  E  A  A  E
N  B  A  R  T  H  O  L  O  M  E  W  D  R
Z  X  M  E  C  I  S  T  B  W  X  S  D  G
T  Y  E  W  U  L  I  H  I  O  A  D  A  S
Q  O  S  T  S  I  M  O  N  P  E  T  E  R
A  P  B  X  H  P  O  M  G  J  T  F  U  U
Z  L  A  S  W  E  N  A  J  A  M  E  S  H
W  S  J  G  S  T  G  S  T  B  U  G  X  Y
M  A  T  T  H  E  W  X  W  W  G  H  B  N
S  X  E  D  C  R  R  F  V  T  G  J  K  L
```

WHO IS GOD?

TODD CAPPS

When you think about God, what do you think about? Do you think about how big He is? Who made Him? What is His purpose?

The Bible helps us know who God is, what He has done, and what He will do in the future. Here are some things to think about.

⊚ God is the one and only true God. Some people believe in more than one god, but there is only one true God. He is God the Father, God the Son, and God the Holy Spirit (the Trinity).

⊚ God has always existed. No one created God. He will live forever.

⊚ God wants you to know who He is. The Bible says to seek God. When you seek something, you look for it. God is everywhere. God sees, hears, and knows everything you do. He is always with you. In fact, God said He will never leave you or turn away from you.

⊚ God wants to have a relationship with you. He created you unique. You are the only "you" in the world. No one else is exactly like you. God sent His Son, Jesus, to provide forgiveness of sin so you can have a relationship with Him. God wants to forgive you of your sins. He wants you to pray and spend time talking and listening to Him.

⊚ God can do anything and everything. No one or no thing can limit God's powers. He has more power than the weather. He controls the sun, moon, and stars. He controls everything that happens. God can do EVERYTHING!

⊚ God told the people who wrote the Bible what to write. As you read the Bible, you will learn more about God. Every verse in the Bible helps you know about God.

⊚ God has special names. Read the names of God on page 42. What do these names tell you about God?

How does it make you feel to know the God who created the universe wants to have a relationship with you? This week you will learn more about God and how He wants to be a part of your life.

DAY 1

GOD IS CREATOR

VERSE OF THE DAY: Genesis 1:1 / CHALLENGE: Genesis 1:1–2:3

 DO! Go outside and count how many things you see, hear, and feel that God created.

How many things did you count? _____

Draw a picture of your favorite items.

KNOW!

✓ God was not created. He has always been and will always be.
✓ God created the world from nothing.
✓ God created the world in six days and rested on the seventh.
✓ God is the creator of all things.
✓ God created a beautiful world for you to enjoy.

PRAY! Thank God for the world He created.

DAY 2

GOD IS ALL-POWERFUL

VERSE OF THE DAY: Deuteronomy 3:24 / CHALLENGE: 1 Kings 18:20-39

DO! What makes something powerful? Rate these things from most powerful (1) to least powerful (5):

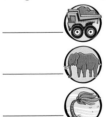

Think about the power of each item. Compare each item to God's power. Which is more powerful, God or the item?

How powerful is God? (Place an X on the line to show how powerful you think God is.)

VERY POWERFUL   NOT POWERFUL

KNOW! Here are just a few things God can do.
✓ Heal (Psalm 30:2)
✓ Protect (Daniel 6:20-21)
✓ Provide (Philippians 4:19)
✓ Answer prayer (Psalm 17:6)
✓ Raise Jesus from the dead (Acts 4:10)
✓ Power to do all things (Mark 10:27)

PRAY! Thank God for His unlimited power.

DAY 3

GOD KNOWS ALL

VERSE OF THE DAY: Psalm 147:5
CHALLENGE: Psalm 139:1-6

 Test your brain:

HOW MANY HAIRS ARE ON YOUR HEAD?

HOW MUCH BLOOD IS IN YOUR BODY?

HOW TALL WILL YOU BE WHEN YOU GROW UP?

Do you know the answers to these questions? God does. He knows everything!

? How do you feel knowing God knows all about you?

? Is there anything you wish God did not know about you?

? Is there anything you need to ask God to forgive you for thinking, saying, or doing?

✓ God knows everything you think, say, and do (Job 36:5).

✓ God knows everywhere you go (Joshua 1:9).

✓ God knows how you treat your friends (Proverbs 17:17).

✓ God knows if you obey your parents (Ephesians 6:1).

✓ God knows when you sin and will forgive you (1 John 1:9).

PRAY Thank God that He knows all things about you. Ask Him to forgive you of things you think, say, and do that do not please Him.

DAY 4

GOD IS THE ONE TRUE GOD

VERSE OF THE DAY: Jeremiah 10:10
CHALLENGE: John 17

 Test your brain:

HOW MANY PEOPLE LIVE IN YOUR CITY?

HOW MANY CARS DO YOU SEE EVERY DAY?

HOW MANY STARS CAN YOU COUNT AT NIGHT?

HOW MANY FRIENDS DO YOU HAVE?

 Are all these numbers more than one? How many things can you list that there is only one of?

✓ The Bible says there is only ONE TRUE GOD (Jeremiah 10:10).

✓ God wants you to obey Him (Jeremiah 7:23).

✓ God wants you to worship Him (Psalm 95:6).

✓ God does not want you to worship other gods (Exodus 20:4).

✓ God wants you to not say His name in ways that disrespect Him (Exodus 20:7).

 Thank God for being the one true God. Ask Him to help you keep Him most important in your life.

DAY 5

GOD IS IN CONTROL

VERSE OF THE DAY: Psalm 93:1 / CHALLENGE: Jonah

DO! If you designed a radio-controlled car or airplane, what would it look like? Draw it here.

KNOW!

✓ God is in control of EVERYTHING.
✓ God gives people the freedom to choose to obey Him or not (Joshua 24:15).
✓ God controls the weather (Psalm 135:7).
✓ God controls the waves in the oceans (Psalm 107:29).
✓ God controls the stars, moon, and sun (Genesis 1:14-19).

PRAY Thank God that He is in control of everything. Ask Him to help you make choices that please and honor Him.

DAY 6

GOD IS PERFECT

VERSE OF THE DAY: Psalm 18:30 / CHALLENGE: Matthew 5:43-48

DO! Find the mistakes in this picture.

How many mistakes have you made this week? Did you learn anything from your mistakes?

KNOW!

✓ God is perfect, He does not make mistakes (Matthew 5:48).
✓ God's ways are perfect (Psalm 18:30).
✓ God's teachings are perfect (Psalm 19:7).
✓ God wants you to be perfect (Matthew 5:48), but because you sin, you are not perfect (Romans 3:23).

PRAY Express appreciation to God that He is perfect. Ask Him to help you follow His perfect plan for your life.

NAMES OF GOD

God is known by many different names in the Bible.
Here are some of God's names.

ADONAI	THE LORDSHIP OF GOD	MALACHI 1:6
EL ELYON	THE MOST HIGH GOD	GENESIS 14:17-20
EL SHADDAI	GOD ALMIGHTY	PSALM 91:1
ELOHIM	POWERFUL GOD	GENESIS 1:1; PSALM 19:1
EL OLAM	THE EVERLASTING GOD	ISAIAH 40:28-31
JEHOVAH JIREH	THE LORD WILL PROVIDE	GENESIS 22:13-14
JEHOVAH MEKADESH	THE LORD THY SANCTIFIER*	EXODUS 31:13
JEHOVAH ROPHE	THE LORD OUR HEALER	EXODUS 15:26
JEHOVAH NISSI	THE LORD OUR BANNER	EXODUS 17:15
JEHOVAH ROHI	THE LORD MY SHEPHERD	PSALM 23:1
JEHOVAH SABAOTH	THE LORD OF HOSTS	ISAIAH 6:1-3
JEHOVAH SHALOM	THE LORD IS PEACE	JUDGES 6:24
JEHOVAH SHAMMAH	THE LORD WHO IS PRESENT	EZEKIEL 48:35
JEHOVAH TSIDKENU	THE LORD OUR RIGHTEOUSNESS	JEREMIAH 23:6
JEHOVAH YAHWEH	THE HOLY GOD	LEVITICUS 19:2

*Sanctifier means the way God works in your life to help you become more like Him.

HEBREW ALPHABET

All of the names of God listed on page 42 come from the Old Testament.
The Old Testament was written in the Hebrew language.

CHECK OUT THE LETTERS OF THE HEBREW ALPHABET.

Aleph (silent)	Bet	Vet	Gimmel	Dalet	Hey	Vav
	b	v	g	d	h	v

Zayin	Chet	Tet	Yod	Kaf	Khaf	Lamed
z	ch (or h)	t	y	k	kh	l

Mem	Nun	Samekh	Ayin (silent)	Pey	Fey	Tsade
m	n	s		p	ph/f	ts/tz

Qof	Resh	Shin	Sin	Tav
q (or k)	r	sh/s	s	t

Practice writing the Hebrew alphabet on a piece of paper.

(Although the alphabet above is written from left to right,
the Hebrew alphabet is read and written from right to left.)

HOW DO I HEAR GOD SPEAK TO ME?

TODD CAPPS

How many people do you talk with every day? Do you remember everything people tell you? Have you ever wondered how God speaks to you? Think about how God spoke to people in Bible times.

- ☻ God spoke to people through prophets.
- ☻ God spoke to people through angels.
- ☻ God spoke to people through dreams.
- ☻ God spoke to people through their thoughts.
- ☻ God spoke to people through other people.

God wants to speak with you. He wants to tell you things. Are you willing to listen to Him? How do you know what you hear is God speaking? Here are some things to keep in mind as you consider if what you hear is God speaking to you:

- ☻ God will never tell you anything that goes against who He is.
- ☻ God will never tell you anything that goes against what He stands for.
- ☻ God will never tell you anything that is not true.
- ☻ God will never tell you anything that is not the best for you.

Learning to listen to God can be difficult. Many things can keep you from listening to God. Your sins, thoughts, desires, dreams, as well as other people can keep you from hearing God. If you are not sure what you hear is from God, ask Him to continue talking with you and help you know for sure what you hear is from Him. This week's Bible studies will help you learn to listen to God more.

DAY 1 — GOD SPEAKS THROUGH THE BIBLE

VERSES OF THE DAY: 2 Timothy 3:15-16
CHALLENGE: Psalm 119:11

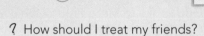 Think about the answers to these questions:

? How should I treat my friends?

? Why should I obey my parents?

? What does God want me to do?

? Why should I pray?

How did you know the answers to these questions?

✓ Studying the Bible helps you know what God wants you to do.
✓ God speaks to you through the Bible.
✓ God gives you examples of how to treat your friends, obey your parents, how to obey Him, and why you should pray.
✓ God speaks to you through His Word, the Bible. The next time you read a Bible verse or story, listen to what God is saying to you.

PRAY Ask God to help you hear Him speak as you read and study your Bible.

DAY 2 — GOD SPEAKS THROUGH PRAYER

VERSE OF THE DAY: 1 Thessalonians 5:17
CHALLENGE: 1 Kings 18:20-46

 Beside the telephones below, write the names of five people or places. Now write the telephone numbers to these people or places. How did you know the numbers? Was it because you call these numbers on a regular basis? How do you feel when you call these phone numbers and get a busy signal or have to leave a voice message?

✓ When you pray, you will never get a busy signal or have to leave a voice message for God.
✓ God hears every time you pray.
✓ God speaks to you and will answer your prayers.

PRAY Ask God to help you hear and understand His voice when He speaks to you.

DAY 3

GOD SPEAKS THROUGH SITUATIONS AND EVENTS IN YOUR LIFE

VERSES OF THE DAY: Exodus 3:1-6 / CHALLENGE: Exodus 3

DO! Write down some things you will do today. How would you know if God spoke to you during one of these events? How would you feel? How would you recognize God's voice?

KNOW! God can speak to you any way He desires.
- ✓ God spoke to Noah and told him to build the ark (Genesis 6:13-22).
- ✓ God spoke to Moses through a burning bush (Exodus 3).
- ✓ God spoke to the people in the Old Testament through prophets (Luke 24:27).
- ✓ God spoke to Mary through the angel Gabriel (Luke 1:26-38).

PRAY God knows about every situation in your life, and He wants to help you. Ask Him to help you know how to handle the situations.

DAY 4

GOD SPEAKS THROUGH PEOPLE

VERSE OF THE DAY: Joshua 3:9 / CHALLENGE: Joshua 3:9-17

DO! Complete the dot to dot. Draw a face to resemble someone you listen to. What are some things people say to you? Does what the people say about God help you know more about Him?

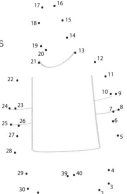

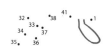

KNOW!
- ✓ In the Bible, God spoke to people through prophets, priests, and people such as Peter, John, and Paul. Who did God speak the most clearly through in the Bible?
- ✓ God speaks through people today. He speaks through your pastor, teachers, parents, and other people. These people must be careful to make sure what they say is really what God says.

PRAY Pray for the people who speak to you about God. Ask God to help the people clearly understand and communicate what God says to them.

DAY 5
GOD SPEAKS THROUGH THE HOLY SPIRIT

VERSE OF THE DAY: John 16:13
CHALLENGE: Acts 2

DO! Use the code below to decode the statement.

__ __ __   __ __ __ __   __ __ __ __ __ __
20 8 5   8 15 12 25   19 16 9 18 9 20

__ __ __ __   __ __ __ __ __ __ __   __ __ __ __ ,
8 5 12 16 19   2 5 12 9 5 22 5 18 19   11 14 15 23

__ __ __ __ __ __ __ __ __ , __ __ __
21 14 4 5 18 19 20 1 14 4   1 14 4

__ __ __ __ __ __ __ __   __ __ __   __ __ __ __ __ __ __
18 5 13 5 13 2 5 18   1 12 12   20 8 9 14 7 19

__ __ __ __ __   __ __ __ .
1 2 15 21 20   7 15 4

KNOW!

✓ The Holy Spirit is a special helper sent by God to help Christians know how to live.
✓ The Holy Spirit helps believers grow in their relationships with God and people.
✓ The Holy Spirit helps people recognize when God is speaking to them.

PRAY Thank God for the Holy Spirit. Ask God to help you listen to and understand what the Holy Spirit says.

DAY 6
GOD SPEAKS THROUGH YOUR THOUGHTS

VERSES OF THE DAY: Romans 12:1-2
CHALLENGE: Psalm 139:2

DO! Read these brain facts.

YOUR BRAIN WEIGHS ABOUT 3 POUNDS.

YOUR BRAIN IS ABOUT 75% WATER.

YOUR BRAIN CANNOT FEEL PAIN.

YOUR BRAIN STOPS GROWING AT AGE 18.

YOUR BRAIN HAS 100,000 MILES OF BLOOD VESSELS.

KNOW!

✓ God knows everything you think (even before you think it).
✓ God wants you to think about things pleasing to Him that will help you.
✓ God speaks to you through your thoughts.
✓ When you feel guilty for thinking something, that is the Holy Spirit telling you to stop thinking about the topic.

PRAY Ask God to help you have thoughts that are positive and pleasing to Him. Ask Him to help you recognize when He is speaking to you through your thoughts.

ADD IT UP!

Place a coin or button on one of the numbered spaces. Select one of the disciple's names in the center of the numbers. Move your coin one space for each letter in the name (you can move your coin in either direction). Write down the number under the coin.

Select another name and move your coin. Add the numbers together. Continue for all 12 names. What is the sum (total) of your numbers? Replay, selecting the names in a different order. Challenge a friend. Who has the greatest total?

ADD IT UP!

Thaddaeus	Matthew
Judas Iscariot	Simon
James	Philip
Andrew	Bartholomew
Simon Peter	Thomas
John	James

A HIDDEN MESSAGE

Cross out every other letter. Write the remaining letters below. What message did you discover?

~~X~~ l b g c r q o w w e c r l t o y s u e i r o t p o a G s o d d f b g y h r j e k a l d z i x n c g v a b n n d m l q e w a e r r n t i y n u g i f o r p o a m s m d y f B g i h b j l k e l .

_ ____ _____ __ ___ __ _____

___ _____ ____ __ _____.

TEST YOUR BIBLE KNOWLEDGE

Read the clues. Use the names in the word bank to fill in the puzzle.

ACROSS

1. _____ was the angel who told Mary she would have a baby. (Luke 1:19)
2. _____ was the disciple who betrayed Jesus. (Matthew 26:47)
3. _____ baptized Jesus. (Matthew 3:13-17)
4. _____ was the second king of Israel. (2 Samuel 5:4)
5. God told _____ to build an ark. (Genesis 6:12-14)
6. _____ was the son of King David and built the temple. (2 Chronicles 3:1)
7. _____ did not listen to God and was swallowed by a big fish. (Jonah 1:17)
8. _____ was the mother of Jesus. (Matthew 2:11)

DOWN

1. _____ climbed a tree so he could see Jesus. (Luke 19:2-9)
2. The first man was named _____. (Genesis 3:17)
3. _____ became the leader of the Israelites after the death of Moses. (Joshua 1:1-5)
4. _____ went with her mother-in-law back to Bethlehem. (Ruth 1:18-19)
5. _____ was the first disciple. (Matthew 4:18-20)
6. _____ would not obey Darius' law. God protected him from the lions. (Daniel 6:1-24)
7. Jesus raised Mary and Martha's brother from the dead. His name was _____. (John 11:38-44)
8. As a baby, _____ was placed in a basket and put in the river by his mother. (Exodus 2:1-10)

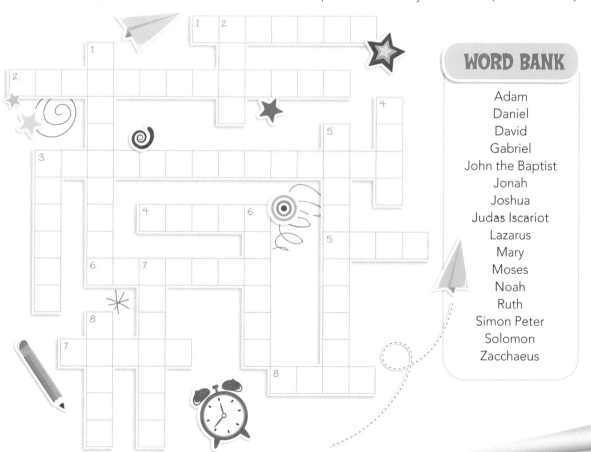

WORD BANK

Adam
Daniel
David
Gabriel
John the Baptist
Jonah
Joshua
Judas Iscariot
Lazarus
Mary
Moses
Noah
Ruth
Simon Peter
Solomon
Zacchaeus

HOW DO I FOLLOW GOD'S PLAN FOR MY LIFE?

RANDY FIELDS

When was the last time you played "Follow the Leader" with a group of friends? Was it easy to follow the leader? Why? Did you try to get people to do some difficult tasks when you were the leader? Did the people follow you? How did you feel when your friends did not follow you? How do you think God feels when people do not follow Him?

Following God's plan for your life is not a game. God has a plan for you and He wants you to follow it. You can trust that God's plan for your life is the best. He wants to help you live a life that is pleasing to Him. You may be asking, "How do I follow God's plan for my life?"

Following God's plan for your life may seem confusing and sometimes even difficult to discover. God wants you to trust Him and His plans. God has given you several tools to help you know His plan and how to follow it.

First, you can **read the Bible.** God tells you everything you need to know in the Bible. He wants you to keep Him first in your life, obey your parents, and live in ways that please and honor Him. All the details on how to do these things and more can be found in the Bible. If you're going to follow God's plan, you must learn to dig in to the Bible and learn what it has to say to you. The Bible tells you what God's plan is for your life.

Second, God wants you to **listen to Him**. You live in a world full of noises and distractions. Sometimes it can be hard to hear God or even know when God is speaking to you. God will tell you what He wants you to do, so be still and listen to Him.

Third, God lets you **ask Him questions**. If you don't know what to do, talk with God. Ask Him to help you really understand what He's saying to you.

Fourth, **talk to your parents, teachers, and pastor.** Hopefully all of these people know how to follow God's plans for their lives. These people can help you know what to do and answer questions about God's plans.

Following God's plan doesn't mean He will send you a map and say "turn here, do this, and don't do that." (He may, but probably not!) You must learn to ask Him what His plan is and be ready to follow it.

You should also know that following God's plan doesn't mean you will never have difficulties. Sometimes God places difficulties in your way to help you grow and to trust Him more. When you face difficult times, ask God, "What are you teaching me through this?" Even in difficult times, do your best to always follow Him. Remember God promised He'll never leave you (Deuteronomy 31:8).

DAY 1

FOLLOW BY LISTENING

VERSE OF THE DAY: John 10:27 / CHALLENGE: Proverbs 8:32-36

DO! Find a quiet place to sit outside. For one minute, close your eyes and listen to everything around you.

LIST HOW MANY DIFFERENT THINGS YOU HEARD.

? What was the easiest thing for you to hear?
? What was the hardest thing for you to hear?
? What made it difficult to listen?

KNOW!

✓ When you belong to Jesus, you will hear and know His voice.
✓ Listening sometimes requires you to be still.
✓ You can hear God speak through the Bible, other people, and circumstances.
    (Review the information you learned on "How Do I Hear God Speak to Me?" pp. 44-47.)

PRAY Ask God to allow you to hear Him. Pray for His guidance in following His plans for you.

DAY 2

FOLLOW BY PRAYING

VERSES OF THE DAY: 1 Thessalonians 5:16-18 / CHALLENGE: Ephesians 6:10-18

DO! Finish these common childhood prayers:

* Now I lay me …

* God is great, God is good, let us …

* Thank You for the world so sweet, thank You …

? What was the very first prayer you learned?

KNOW!

✓ Prayers such as these are good to help you get started, but God wants you to move beyond these simple prayers.
✓ You can use your own words when you pray.
✓ Ask God to show you His plan for your life. He's not keeping a secret that He doesn't want you to know.
✓ God will probably not show you everything about your life, but He'll show you what you need to know right now.

PRAY Ask God to show you what you should be doing right now.

DAY 3
FOLLOW BY ASKING

VERSES OF THE DAY: Matthew 7:7-8
CHALLENGE: Matthew 6:25-34

DO! Ask three people to give you directions to the library or grocery store.

? What were the people's responses?

Did you get different answers from people even though the question was the same? Why?

Make a list of questions you would like to ask God about His plans for your life.

✓ People see things differently and as a result, give different responses when asked questions.
✓ The first step to following God's plan is to ask Him to show you what to do.
✓ The Bible tells you to ask God and He will show you.

PRAY Read your list of questions to God. Listen as He responds. Thank God for the freedom you have to ask Him questions.

DAY 4
FOLLOW BY FOLLOWING THE LEADER

VERSES OF THE DAY: 1 Peter 2:21-25
CHALLENGE: Matthew 6:33-34

DO!

TOUCH YOUR TOES 3 TIMES.   RUN IN PLACE FOR 2 MINUTES.   COMPLETE 10 JUMPING JACKS.

Did you do these exercises? Would you have been more motivated to do them if someone was standing in front of you making you do the exercises? Why?

What are some things you learned by following someone else's example?

✓ The best way to learn what it means to follow God's plan is to read about the examples Jesus gave you.
✓ Jesus followed God's plan for His life. He left heaven and came to earth just like God planned.
✓ Jesus willingly suffered on the cross, died, and was resurrected to fulfill God's plan for His life.
✓ Following God's plan for your life is a choice. God will not force you to follow His plan.
✓ God knows what is best for you. He has a great plan for you, if you will follow the Leader, His Son, Jesus.

PRAY Thank God for the example Jesus provided. Ask God to help you be obedient like Jesus.

FOLLOW BY DIGGING IN TO GOD'S WORD

DAY 5

VERSES OF THE DAY: 2 Timothy 3:16-17 / CHALLENGE: Matthew 13:3-9,18-23

DO! Search for tools used for digging and drilling.

```
V  Q  V  F  Z  D  B  D  V  W  L  R  E  P  N
W  R  E  N  C  H  R  I  N  N  C  E  O  P  N
S  Z  L  K  U  L  S  O  B  O  N  Z  H  A  L
P  W  E  R  E  P  T  A  W  L  R  A  K  E  F
T  P  Q  V  A  K  Z  W  E  S  E  E  C  O  S
F  X  O  D  I  Z  C  Z  D  H  D  K  A  W  A
A  H  E  G  U  D  R  I  L  L  X  O  B  Y  I
S  F  J  S  R  Q  E  Q  P  I  M  E  G  Y  O
```

WORD BANK

Backhoe	Pick	Shovel	Wrench
Drill	Rake	Spade	

Think about tools you use to help you dig deeper in to the Bible. You can use Bible dictionaries, concordances, and maps to help you learn more about the events in the Bible.

✓ God speaks through His Word, the Bible.
✓ Studying God's Word can help you discover His plan for your life.
✓ The more you study, the clearer God's plan for your life becomes.

PRAY Ask God to help you build a habit of studying His Word each day.

FOLLOW BY PRESSING ON

DAY 6

VERSES OF THE DAY: Philippians 3:13-14 / CHALLENGE: Hebrews 10:35-36

DO! How many pairs of shoes do you own?

> DRAW A PICTURE OF YOUR FAVORITE PAIR OF SHOES.

What is the farthest distance you have ever run? Did you get tired and want to quit? Why?

✓ Walking in God's will and following His plan is what He wants you to do for the rest of your life.
✓ You will get tired and be tempted to look back at where you came from. You may wish to stop walking (following) God's plan, but DON'T. Keep going! Keep pressing on!
✓ No matter how hard life gets, if you keep on following God, you will make it to the finish line.

PRAY Ask God to help you follow His plans even when things get difficult and you want to quit.

FIX THE LETTERS

Write the letter that comes after
the one printed to discover some special messages.

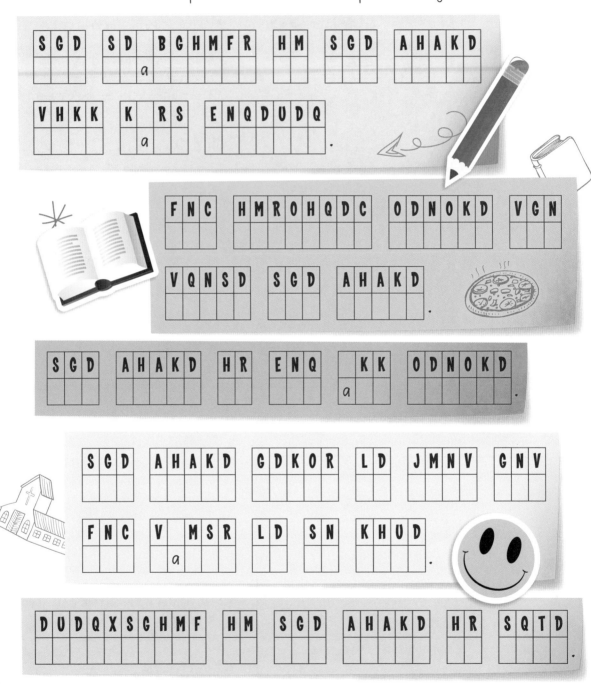

S G D   **S D**   **B G H M F R**   **H M**   **S G D**   **A H A K D**
(second cell of "S D": _a_)

V H K K   **K**   **R S**   **E N Q D U D Q** .
(second cell of "K": _a_)

F N C   **H M R O H Q D C**   **O D N O K D**   **V G N**

V Q N S D   **S G D**   **A H A K D** .

S G D   **A H A K D**   **H R**   **E N Q**   **K K**   **O D N O K D** .
(under "K K": _a_)

S G D   **A H A K D**   **G D K O R**   **L D**   **J M N V**   **G N V**

F N C   **V**   **M S R**   **L D**   **S N**   **K H U D** .
(second cell of "V": _a_)

D U D Q X S G H M F   **H M**   **S G D**   **A H A K D**   **H R**   **S Q T D** .

ABCDEFGHIJKLMNOPQRSTUVWXYZ

WHAT'S MISSING?

Look at the names of these Bible books.
Fill in the names of the missing Bible books.

HOW DO I USE MY TALENTS AND ABILITIES TO SERVE GOD?

VICKI HULSEY

Has anyone ever told you that you are special? Did you believe her? You should—it's true! The Bible says God made you special. No one else is like you. God even gave you talents and abilities (gifts God gives people to serve Him). What are some of your talents and abilities? Can you play a musical instrument or teach someone how to do something like cook, sing, or run really fast? Take a few minutes to think about the gifts God has given you.

God has a special plan for your life. A part of God's plan for you as a Christian is to be an active part of the church. The church is made up of Christians who have been baptized and who are willing to work together and use their talents and abilities to serve God. Here are just a few ways people use their talents and abilities at church: singing, playing musical instruments, teaching, cooking, cleaning, speaking, leading recreation, and acting. Can you think of some other ways?

You may be wondering *I'm just a kid. Can God use me now, or do I have to wait until I grow up?* God wants to use you RIGHT NOW! What does it mean to serve God? Serving God means you use your talents and abilities to praise God as well as help other people know about Him. For example, if you can play the piano, you may play a song that helps you think about who God is. You can do this at home or in your church's worship service. You can also use your speaking ability to tell someone about God. No matter how young or old a person is, God wants the person to serve Him. Think about how you can use your talents and abilities to serve this week.

Here's some other information to help you understand talents and abilities.

- God has given every Christian talents and abilities to use in serving Him and others.
- God is pleased when you use your talents and abilities by helping others.
- God wants you to be happy about serving Him. He is pleased when you have a good attitude about serving.
- Serving God means helping Him. God has work for you to do. He wants you to use the talents and abilities He gave you to help others learn about Him.
- Part of using your talents and abilities means doing things for other people. God will help you learn what He has for you to do.
- As a church member, you need to do your part in serving God. The church needs EVERYONE using his talents and abilities.
- Jesus served others. He made sick people well, gave food to people who were hungry, and even washed the disciples' feet. Jesus was glad to help others.
- Jesus served others without expecting anything in return. Jesus served because of His love for God and people.

DAY 1 — ONE OF A KIND!

VERSE OF THE DAY: Ephesians 2:10
CHALLENGE: Psalm 139:13-18

 Circle the things you are good at doing.

SPEAKING   DRAWING
PLAYING MUSICAL INSTRUMENTS
PLAYING SPORTS
SINGING
TEACHING
SEWING   DANCING

In what ways can you serve God through these activities?

Think of your two best friends. Are they exactly like you? What talents and abilities do they have?

KNOW!

✓ God gave you talents and abilities to serve Him.
✓ Each person has different talents and abilities.
✓ God does not expect you to be perfect when using your gifts, but He does expect you to use them.

PRAY
Thank God for giving you talents and abilities that you can use to serve Him. Specifically name each talent and ability you have. Ask God to help you learn how to use your gifts to help people know more about Him.

DAY 2 — TEAMWORK!

VERSE OF THE DAY: Romans 12:5
CHALLENGE: Romans 12:1-8

 What is your favorite team? What would happen if one player decided to play all of the positions? Would the team win? How important is teamwork?

Make a list of the different jobs people do in your church.

How do these jobs help you worship and learn about God?

Could one person do all of these jobs by himself? No! Everyone needs to work together.

KNOW!

✓ The church is more than a building, the church is Christians who do God's work.
✓ Church members have different responsibilities.
✓ As a church member, you need to do your part in serving God.

PRAY
 Thank God for the people in your church who willingly use their talents and abilities.

DAY 3

NOT TOO YOUNG!

VERSE OF THE DAY: 1 Timothy 4:12 / CHALLENGE: 1 Timothy 4:11-16

DO! What are some things that adults can do, but you cannot?

OK, so there are some things that you have to wait to do, but serving God is not one of them.

Think about the talents and abilities God has given you. List five of them. Write how you can use your gifts to serve.

KNOW!

✓ Your church provides ways for you to help other people.
✓ You are not too young to use your talents and abilities.

PRAY Ask God to give you opportunities to use your talents and abilities.

MY TALENTS AND ABILITIES

HOW I CAN USE THESE GIFTS

DAY 4

JESUS IS MY EXAMPLE!

VERSE OF THE DAY: Matthew 20:28 / CHALLENGE: John 13:4-17

DO! Draw a picture of you in the left-hand box. Draw a picture of Jesus in the right-hand box. Read each statement. Check if the statement applies to you, Jesus, or both.

ME		JESUS
○	Likes to spend time with people	○
○	Prays for people	○
○	Uses talents and abilities to help people	○
○	Encourages people	○
○	Obeys God	○

KNOW!

✓ Jesus is your example for how you treat other people.
✓ You follow Jesus' example when you obey God.

PRAY Ask God to help you become more like Jesus as you use your talents and abilities.

How do you compare to Jesus? What talents and abilities did He have while on earth? Jesus is the perfect example of how to live a life that pleases and honors God. What do you need to do to become more like Jesus? How can using your talents and abilities help others?

DAY 5

ATTITUDE CHECK!

VERSE OF THE DAY: Ephesians 6:7
CHALLENGE: Psalm 100

DO! Number these chores from your least to most favorite.

What kind of attitude do you have when doing these chores? What does your attitude say about you? Did you know you are serving God when you serve your family? You don't have to be at church to use your talents and abilities.

KNOW!

√ God wants you to treat your family members fairly and with kindness.
√ You can use your talents and abilities ANYWHERE and ANYTIME.
√ God wants your actions, attitudes, and words to be pleasing to Him.

PRAY Ask God to help you have a good attitude about serving your family.

DAY 6

WATCH YOUR PRIDE

VERSE OF THE DAY: Proverbs 11:2
CHALLENGE: Proverbs 29:23

DO! What are some things you think you do better than anyone else? Why do you feel this way? Color in all of the 1s.

Pride is "too high an opinion of one's own ability or worth." That means you think you're better at doing something than someone else.

When you use your talents and abilities, do not think you're better than anyone else. You can feel good about what you do, but don't focus on what people think about your talents. Focus on what God thinks.

KNOW!

√ God wants you to do your best.
√ God is not pleased when you brag about what you can do.
√ God gives you talents and abilities to glorify Him, not yourself.

PRAY Ask God to help you use your talents and abilities for His glory, not your own.

HOW DO I USE MY TALENTS AND ABILITIES TO SERVE GOD? 59

SPIRITUAL GIFTS

God gives every Christian talents and abilities to use to serve Him and others.
Look at six gifts God gives people. Read the information about the gifts.
Circle ways you can use these gifts this week. Write in additional ways people can
use these gifts. Which gifts do you think God has given you?

TEACHING

God gives this gift to some Christians so they can help others learn new things.

→ Help a preschooler learn to write his name
→ Teach a song to someone
→ Show your brother how to play a video game
→ Teach a group of children
→ Explain how to do math

_____

_____

SERVING

God gives this gift to some Christians to help meet the needs of people or help them do things.

→ Take clothes to a shelter
→ Clean an area of the church
→ Decorate bulletin boards
→ Plant flowers for someone
→ Wash dishes
→ Fold laundry

_____

_____

ENCOURAGING

God gives this gift to some Christians so they can say words of comfort to help make others feel better.

→ Write a note or letter to someone
→ Send an e-mail telling someone he did a good job
→ Spend time with an elderly neighbor
→ Say, "Good job" to someone at school

_____

_____

HELPING OTHERS

God gives this gift to some Christians to help people going through difficult times.

→ Rake leaves for someone
→ Prepare and deliver food to someone who is sick
→ Spend time talking with someone
→ Make get-well cards for people in the hospital

HOSPITALITY

God gives this gift to some Christians so they can help people feel loved and welcomed.

→ Serve a meal at a homeless shelter
→ Gather and deliver clothing
→ Make gift baskets for new people in the community

ADMINISTRATION

God gives this gift to some Christians so they understand how to get things done.

→ Clean out and organize a storage room
→ Plan a class party
→ Prepare a checklist of items to be completed

*Adapted from *Talent Search* by Hope Winter, LifeWay Press, ©2000.

WHAT HAPPENS WHEN I SIN AGAIN?

RANDY FIELDS

What is something you enjoy doing over and over again? Maybe it's riding a bike, swimming, reading, sewing, learning to play a musical instrument, or learning a new computer skill. Do you discover you get better at doing these things the more you do them? Living in ways that please and honor God takes practice as well. When you became a Christian, you became a new person. All of your sins were forgiven, but that doesn't mean you will never sin again. In fact, the Bible never promises that you'll not sin again after becoming a Christian. So, what happens when you sin again?

The Bible has a lot to say about sin and how it affects people. In the Old Testament, people made sacrifices for the forgiveness of their sins. In the New Testament, Jesus became the ultimate sacrifice for sin. Check out these facts about sin:

- Everyone has sinned (Romans 3:23).
- The payment (wages) of sin is death (Romans 6:23).
- Jesus died for you while you were still a sinner (Romans 5:8).
- God forgives sin EVERY time you ask Him (1 John 1:9).
- God gives people the freedom to choose to live by a sinful nature or to accept forgiveness through Christ (Colossians 1:14).
- Good works and trying to live a perfect life do not provide forgiveness of sin (Ephesians 2:8-9).
- By saying you have not sinned, YOU SINNED (1 John 1:8).
- You can work on becoming more like Christ so you can sin less (Romans 6:4).
- Memorizing Bible verses and living them out will help you sin less (Psalm 119:11).
- God knows and understands all the temptations you face, yet He has the power to overcome them (1 Corinthians 10:13).
- Do not put yourself in places where you will be tempted to sin (1 Corinthians 10:6-14).

As a Christian, when you do sin it is important to confess what you did, ask God to forgive you, and try not to repeat the action. Remember—YOU WILL SIN. God does not love the sin in your life, but He will NEVER stop loving you.

DAY 1

REALIZE IT'S GOING TO HAPPEN!

VERSES OF THE DAY: Romans 6:11-18 / CHALLENGE: Colossians 2:9-15

DO! Locate a picture of your mother and father. Circle who you look like most.

MOTHER   FATHER

→ List some of the characteristics you inherited from your mom or dad.

→ List anything you wish you had not inherited from your mom and dad.

✓ God created people with the ability to make choices. You have the ability to choose to or reject sin.

✓ Everyone sins!

✓ When you became a Christian, you became a different person. Christ lives in you and wants you to stop sinning.

✓ You will sin again, but God still loves you and will forgive you.

PRAY Thank God that He loves you so much He is willing to forgive you. Tell God all of the sins you did and ask Him to forgive you and help you not repeat the sins.

DAY 2

SEARCH AND DESTROY

VERSE OF THE DAY: Psalm 32:5 / CHALLENGE: Psalm 139:1-24

DO! Who is your favorite superhero? Which of these actions can your superhero accomplish?

☐ Knows everything a person does
☐ Sees everything a person does
☐ Knows everything a person thinks
☐ Is everywhere at the same time
☐ Is the most powerful person in the universe
☐ Defeats sin in the world

Can your superhero do these things? GOD CAN! In fact, God does these things every day.

✓ God knows EVERYTHING you do (both good and bad).

✓ God wants you to admit what you did and ask Him to forgive you.

✓ God knows what you think. He wants you to think good things about Him and people.

✓ God defeated Satan when Jesus died on the cross and rose again.

PRAY Ask God to search your life (what you think, how you act, and how you obey Him) and help you see if there is anything you have not confessed. Once He has shown you these things, ask Him to forgive you.

DAY 3

BUILD UP YOUR STRENGTH

VERSE OF THE DAY: Psalm 119:11
CHALLENGE: Colossians 3:1-14

→ Locate the heaviest thing you can lift with one arm.
→ Lift the item five times with each arm. How did it make your arms feel?
→ Check the ways you work to build up the muscles in your body.
☐ Eat healthy foods
☐ Get plenty of sleep
☐ Exercise every day
☐ _____
☐ _____

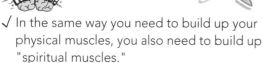

KNOW!

✓ In the same way you need to build up your physical muscles, you also need to build up "spiritual muscles."
✓ Building up spiritual muscles gives you the strength to stop giving in to sin.
✓ God instructs you to hide (memorize) His Word, the Bible, in your heart or mind so you will not sin.
✓ Your muscles have memories. When you build up your physical muscles, they remember what they are supposed to do and work better. The same thing happens with your "spiritual muscles." Memorizing Bible verses and putting them into practice helps you live in ways that please and honor God.
✓ Like a bodybuilder, you must learn what to put into your body and what to get rid of so you can be strong and not give in to sin.

PRAY Ask God to help you memorize Bible verses so you can build up your spiritual strength.

DAY 4

POWER UP!

VERSE OF THE DAY: 1 Corinthians 10:13
CHALLENGE: 1 Peter 4:1-11

 DO! What makes something powerful? How powerful are you?
Number the items from least to most powerful.

Why did you number the items in this order?
If you were describing the power of these items to a friend, how would you describe them?

KNOW!

✓ As a Christian, you've been given the power to overcome temptation and the sin that follows.
✓ Jesus defeated sin so you can have the power to stand up against it.
✓ No temptation exists that you do not have the power to overcome.
✓ God promised He will always provide a way of escape when you're tempted to sin.
✓ You need to depend on God's power and not your own to overcome temptation.
✓ Know it is easy to say you trust God's power, but may be difficult to do so (many times it is easier to give in to the temptation than stand up for what you know God wants you to do).

PRAY Thank God that He gave you the power needed to overcome temptation and sin.

DAY 5

BE SMART, DON'T START

VERSES OF THE DAY: PSALM 1 / CHALLENGE: 1 PETER 5:8-9

 DO! Spend some time observing other kids for a few minutes, then answer these questions.

? What are some behaviors you saw?

? Do you consider these behaviors good or bad? Why?

? What are some ways you can avoid starting bad habits?

KNOW!

✓ Be alert and watch out for situations that can cause you to sin. Try to avoid these situations if at all possible. If you cannot avoid the situations, ask God to help you know what to do.
✓ Watch your friends. Do your friends help you make right choices? Do they try to live in ways that please and honor God?

PRAY Ask God to give you the wisdom to make wise choices. Pray for your friends to have the courage to obey God as well.

DAY 6

IF YOU FALL, GET BACK UP

VERSES OF THE DAY: Hebrews 12:4-6 / CHALLENGE: Galatians 6:6-9

DO! What happened the first time you tried to:

RIDE A BIKE

RIDE A SKATEBOARD

BAKE A CAKE

PLAY AN INSTRUMENT

What would have happened if you quit trying to learn any of these things every time you did not succeed?

 KNOW!

✓ Living in ways that please and honor God takes time. You will make mistakes, but don't give up.
✓ God wants you to keep trying to obey Him.
✓ God knows you'll sin again, but He promises to forgive and help you.

PRAY Ask God to give you the desire to never give up doing the right thing.

HOW THE BIBLE CAN HELP ME

The Bible can help me when I am ...

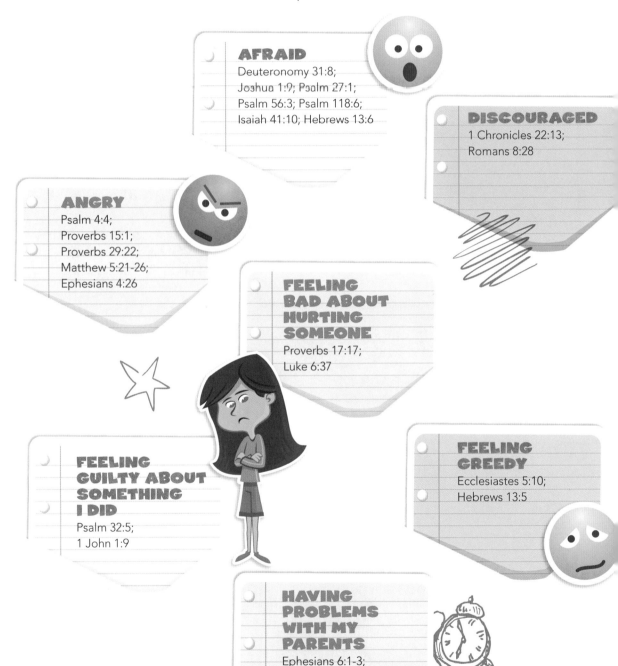

AFRAID
Deuteronomy 31:8;
Joshua 1:9; Psalm 27:1;
Psalm 56:3; Psalm 118:6;
Isaiah 41:10; Hebrews 13:6

DISCOURAGED
1 Chronicles 22:13;
Romans 8:28

ANGRY
Psalm 4:4;
Proverbs 15:1;
Proverbs 29:22;
Matthew 5:21-26;
Ephesians 4:26

FEELING BAD ABOUT HURTING SOMEONE
Proverbs 17:17;
Luke 6:37

FEELING GUILTY ABOUT SOMETHING I DID
Psalm 32:5;
1 John 1:9

FEELING GREEDY
Ecclesiastes 5:10;
Hebrews 13:5

HAVING PROBLEMS WITH MY PARENTS
Ephesians 6:1-3;
Colossians 3:20

NEEDING TO KNOW GOD'S WILL
Proverbs 3:5-6;
Jeremiah 29:11;
Matthew 6:31

TEMPTED TO LIE
Leviticus 19:11;
Psalm 34:13;
Matthew 19:18;
Colossians 3:9

SICK
Exodus 15:26;
Jeremiah 17:14

TEMPTED
Matthew 26:41;
1 Corinthians 10:13

TEMPTED TO BE SELFISH
Psalm 119:36;
Philippians 2:3;
1 John 4:7-8

TEMPTED TO GET BACK AT SOMEONE WHO HURT ME
Leviticus 19:18;
Romans 12:17-21

WORRIED
Matthew 6:25-34;
Matthew 10:19;
Philippians 4:6,19

SAD
Psalm 55:22;
John 14:27;
1 Peter 5:7

WHAT IS WORSHIP?
WHEN AND HOW SHOULD I WORSHIP?

ALISON CREEL

Worship—Giving honor, reverence, and praise to God; the response of people to God.

Do you worship? In what ways do you give honor, reverence, and praise to God?

Worship is not just a feeling or a thought, it is an ACTION—something you do to honor God. God wants you to worship Him. The Bible says God is happy when you worship and that your worship is pleasing (Psalm 149:1-5).

God created you to be a worshiper! He wants to have a relationship with you, that's why He sent His Son, Jesus. God's desire is for all people to accept His forgiveness for sin and spend eternity (forever) worshiping Him.

Before you can worship God, you have to know Him. You get to know God by reading the Bible, praying, going to church, and learning from your parents and teachers. The more you know about God, the more *reasons* you have to worship Him. The more you know God, the more you *want* to worship Him. When you make God the most important part of your life, you will want to make choices that please Him, including worship.

God loves when you worship Him all by yourself, but He also wants you to worship with other Christians. The Bible encourages believers to meet together (Hebrews 10:25). The church is a group of baptized Christians who meet together to pray, tell others about Jesus, worship God, learn from the Bible, meet needs of people, and encourage one another. These actions are ways people express their worship.

Worship is not something you only do on Sundays or at church (Matthew 15:8-9). Worship is your whole life! You can worship any day of the week, at any time of the day. You can also worship ANYWHERE—school, dance, playground, or camping. God provided a beautiful world for you to enjoy. You can worship Him as you enjoy the things He created.

How can you worship? Worship can take many different forms. One of the most common ways of worship is by singing songs, but you can also read Bible verses, pray, dance, clap your hands, lift your hands, sit quietly, serve others, or listen to music as well. These are just a few ways people worship. Worship is whatever you do to tell God how awesome He is and agreeing there is nothing more important than Him.

DAY 1

WHAT IS WORSHIP?

VERSE OF THE DAY: Revelation 4:11
CHALLENGE: Psalm 95:1-7

 Search your room for three of your most special treasures. List or draw pictures of the items on the treasure chest.

What makes your treasures special? Why are they worth so much to you? Think about God. How much is God worth to you? Is He more special than anything else in your life?

Spend a few minutes thinking about God. Think about how much He loves you, how special He is, and about your relationship with Him.

KNOW
✓ Worship is expressing how important God is to you.
✓ Worship is an action.
✓ God is worthy of praise and worship.
✓ Jesus taught that worship is focusing on God alone.

PRAY Tell God how special He is and why He is worth so much to you.

DAY 2

WHY SHOULD I WORSHIP?

VERSE OF THE DAY: PSALM 96:9
CHALLENGE: PSALM 99

 Locate and read these verses in your Bible. Match the verses to the correct descriptions about God.

God is everywhere ∘
God never gets tired ∘
God is always faithful ∘
God can do anything ∘
God is always truthful ∘

∘ Jeremiah 32:17
∘ Proverbs 30:5
∘ Psalm 139:7-10
∘ 2 Timothy 2:13
∘ Isaiah 40:28

Spend time thinking about these characteristics of God. Tell God how thankful you are for who God is. Focus on God, not yourself.

KNOW
✓ The Bible instructs you to worship (Psalm 95:6-7; Matthew 4:9-10).
✓ Worship helps you grow closer to God.
✓ Worship should be your primary way of expressing love to God (1 Peter 1:8).
✓ God is the only person worthy of worship (1 Chronicles 16:25).
✓ God wants you to worship Him with other people as well as by yourself.

PRAY Close your eyes and sit still. Focus on who God is. Sing songs of praise as your prayer.

DAY 3

HOW SHOULD I WORSHIP?

VERSE OF THE DAY: Matthew 22:37 / CHALLENGE: Psalm 150

DO! Can you complete the Sudoku puzzle? Each way of worship should appear only once in every row, column, and square.

What do these actions have to do with worship?

KNOW! God wants you to not just sing words or go through other actions, He wants you to really mean what you say and do.

✓ The Bible is full of examples of how you can worship:
 * Sing (Psalm 100:2)
 * Pray (1 Thessalonians 5:17)
 * Dance (Psalm 149:3)
 * Give (Isaiah 58:7)
 * Serve (Matthew 4:10)
✓ Remember—how you worship begins with ATTITUDE.

PRAY Ask God to help you have the right attitude when you worship.

DAY 4

WHEN SHOULD I WORSHIP?

VERSE OF THE DAY: Philippians 4:4 / CHALLENGE: Daniel 6:1-10

DO! Use the clock to solve the code.

KNOW!

✓ God is not limited by time or place. He wants you to worship Him all the time (morning, noon, afternoon, and evening).
✓ God wants the things you do to be a part of your worship of Him. Everything you do should praise God.

PRAY Thank God that you can worship Him any time.

Write the times you do these things:

_____ Get up	_____ Go to school	_____ Eat lunch
_____ Eat dinner	_____ Go to bed	_____ Worship

DAY 5
WHO SHOULD I WORSHIP?

VERSES OF THE DAY: Exodus 20:3-5
CHALLENGE: 1 Kings 18:20-39

DO!
→ Cross out the names ending in the letter R.
→ Cross out the names of people you play sports or study with.
→ Cross out the names of people you live with.
→ Cross out the names of people elected to leadership positions.
→ Cross out any names with more than three letters.

What name is left? This is the Person you should worship.

SISTER
PARENTS
GOD
BROTHER
FRIEND
TEACHER
PASTOR
CLASSMATES
TEAMMATES
GOVERNMENT LEADERS

✓ God wants you to worship only Him.
✓ Some people believe in more than one god, but there is only one true God (Isaiah 43:10).
✓ God is the creator of all things. He is worthy of your worship.

PRAY Thank God for the freedom you have to worship Him.

DAY 6
WHERE SHOULD I WORSHIP?

VERSE OF THE DAY: 1 Corinthians 3:16
CHALLENGE: Acts 17:24-25

DO! Doctors use special tools to see things inside of you. Sometimes doctors use x-rays to look at your bones and other parts of your body. Stand in front of a mirror and open your mouth as wide as possible. Use a flashlight to look in your mouth. What do you see? Draw a picture of what you saw.

What does God see when He looks inside of you? Does He see someone who is ready to worship Him?

✓ Worship is not limited to a place. You can worship in a church building, school bus, doctor's office, playground, or where you are right now. You can worship ANYWHERE!
✓ The Bible teaches that your body is God's temple (1 Corinthians 3:16). A *temple* is "a place of worship." Worship doesn't just happen at church; it's a part of who you are!
✓ You can worship God privately (Jeremiah 29:13).
✓ You can worship with other believers (Psalm 149:1).

PRAY Ask God to help you worship wherever you are.

HOW TO PREPARE YOUR CHILD FOR WORSHIP

OK—you found one of the pages your parents need to read. Take your *I'm a Christian, Now What?* journal to your parents and ask them to read this page.

Deuteronomy 6:4-9 instructs parents to teach their children. Take a minute and read these verses. Notice the teaching did not occur in a church. The verses teach that spiritual training was to occur throughout daily life. Parents have the responsibility to live out their beliefs for their children. In applying these verses to worship, it is important that parents model worship for their children at home and in corporate worship services. Here are some tips to help you prepare your child to worship.

- Accept the God-given responsibility of guiding your child to worship.
- Talk with your child about worship. Ask him to define worship. Discuss and expound on your child's definition. Talk about how people worship, the purpose of worship, and how your family worships.
- Remember your child will learn the importance of worship as you model it. Worshiping as a family brings families together.
- Seek to set positive examples and maintain positive attitudes about worshiping with your child.
- Maintain regular attendance and be on time to corporate worship services.
- Participate with your child through singing, reading the Bible, giving offerings, and praying.
- Remember your child's developmental characteristics. Sitting still for long periods of time is not developmentally appropriate for younger children.
- Sit where your child can see and hear during the worship service.
- Pray for and with your child before, during, and after the worship experience.
- Worship with your child during the week by including conversations about God in everyday life, singing praise songs, and expressing gratitude to God for the things He does.
- Decide what clothes to wear to church on Saturday afternoon. Gather all shoes, socks, and other clothing.
- Ensure your child is well-rested and eats a nourishing breakfast on Sunday morning.
- Provide times for your child to get to know the church staff.
- Allow your child to take a "Big Church" bag with crayons, paper, and chenille stems to worship.
- Encourage your child to listen for familiar names, words, or events during the worship time.
- Comment on your child's behavior following the worship service.
- Ask/Answer questions related to the songs, sermon, and other things your child experienced.

HOW TO TAKE NOTES DURING WORSHIP

Have you ever heard someone say, "Let me write that down so I don't forget it"? How did writing something down help the person recall the information?

Let's see how well you do at remembering. Imagine that your mom asked you and your dad to go to the grocery store. Here's the list of things your mom wants you to buy.

Milk
Cheese
Strawberries
Orange Juice
Ice Cream
Pickles
Lunch meat
Bread
Lettuce
Eggs

Read over the list three times. You may even say the items out loud. Now, turn your journal over and name the items.

How did you do? Did you remember all 10 items? What if you had written the items down, do you think that would have helped you remember them? Try it!

Writing things down helps you remember them better. Here are some helps in learning what to write.

- Write down key (important) thoughts—don't try to write down everything, summarize what you hear.
- Write down words you don't understand—locate the words in a dictionary and discover what they mean after the worship time.
- Don't worry about writing complete sentences.
- Write things in your own words.
- Don't worry about spelling things correctly, try to spell as best you can so you can remember the words (you can rewrite the notes later).
- Practice taking notes—the more you do it, the easier it will become.

Pages 100-105 provide you space to take worship notes. Take your *I'm a Christian, Now What?* journal with you to worship. Take notes of what your pastor says. After the worship service, respond to the four statements. During the week, look back over your notes. Are you applying the worship notes to your life?

WHAT IS AN OFFERING? WHY SHOULD I TITHE?

AMY GRUBB

When you attend someone's birthday party, what do you take? A gift! At Christmas, what do you give people? Gifts! Everyone likes to receive presents, but why do you give them?

Giving someone a gift is a way to show that you care about her. You might give someone a gift to honor her or to say thank you for doing something special. You might give a gift to demonstrate (show) your love for someone. You may even give a surprise gift, not letting the person know who the gift is from.

Think about things you give or receive as gifts. Often gifts are purchased with money, but sometimes they might be homemade. Spending time with someone or sharing your talents can also be gifts. What are some gifts you have given people? How did the gifts make the person who received them feel?

An *offering* is "a gift people give God." Your offering to God might be money you give at church, time you spend serving others, or telling someone about God. Some people are confused when they hear, "Give God your offering," but they do not see God. The money you give at church is used for the various ministries your church provides. Giving your money to the church is the same as giving it to God.

A *tithe* is a special kind of offering where people "give one-tenth of their money, crops, or property to God." God gave the Israelites a law requiring them to give one-tenth of their possessions (the things they own) to Him (Leviticus 27:30,32). Jesus encouraged His followers to tithe and to have a good attitude about giving (Matthew 23:23).

You might wonder why God needs your gifts. The truth is—He DOESN'T. After all, He created everything! So, why should you tithe or give an offering? As a Christian, you should follow the instructions in the Bible. The Bible is God's message to you and teaches you how to live the Christian life. The Bible instructs Christians to tithe out of obedience to God's laws. By bringing an offering to God, you honor Him and show Him that you love Him. God deserves respect, obedience, and honor.

By giving back one-tenth of the incredible blessings God has given you, you can be obedient to Him, honor Him, and receive additional blessings! Who wouldn't want to tithe?!

DAY 1

FIRST THINGS FIRST

VERSE OF THE DAY: Proverbs 3:9 / CHALLENGE: Psalm 24:1-2

DO! How many of these items do you own?

Who gave you these things? What do these gifts tell you about how people feel about you?

KNOW!

✓ God gave you the gift of His Son, Jesus, to pay the penalty for your sins. God loves you that much!
✓ You can honor God by giving offerings of money, things you own, or time.
✓ God wants your best, not your leftovers!
✓ Giving to God demonstrates (shows) your love and thankfulness for what He does for you.

PRAY Ask God to show you how you can honor Him with your possessions (things you own).

DAY 2

GOD OWNS IT ALL!

VERSE OF THE DAY: 1 Chronicles 29:11 / CHALLENGE: 1 Chronicles 29:11-14

DO!

→ Locate the word *one* on the center back of a dollar bill. What words are written above the word?

_____

→ Find a penny, nickle, dime, and quarter. What four words regarding God are on each coin?

_____

_____

_____

_____

KNOW!

✓ God created everything from nothing.
✓ God owns everything. He does not need you to give things back to Him, but He wants you to.
✓ God wants people to give offerings to help them show their love and honor to Him.
✓ Giving offerings shows obedience to God.

PRAY Thank God for all of the many things He has given you.

DAY 3

CHECK YOUR ATTITUDE

VERSES OF THE DAY: 2 Corinthians 9:6-8
CHALLENGE: Philippians 2:5-11

DO! Take a few minutes to look at the photos in your home. Do you know all these people? Looking at the expressions on their faces, what type of attitude do you think they had? Why?

Which face best describes the statements? Draw a line from each statement to a face.

"I just received a gift."

"I need to give my offering."

"My mom says I should tithe on my birthday money."

"I worked for my money. It's all mine!"

What does the Bible say about the type of attitude you should have when you give?

✓ God wants you to obey Him and give Him your offerings, but He wants you to have a good attitude about giving.
✓ Being a church member involves responsibilities and privileges. One responsibility church members have is to give offerings and tithes.
✓ God knows your attitude. You may smile and make people think you are happy when you are not, but God knows the truth. ·

PRAY Ask God to help you have a positive, cheerful attitude when giving.

DAY 4

MORE THAN MATH

VERSES OF THE DAY: Deuteronomy 14:22-23
CHALLENGE: Leviticus 27:30

DO! Shade in one-tenth of the dollar bill and coins.

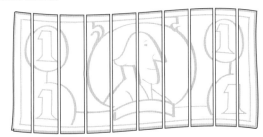

If you had a dollar bill, one-tenth would equal 10¢.

✓ A tithe is an offering of one-tenth.
✓ Abram gave the first tithe to honor God after God saved him from his enemies (Genesis 14:18-20).
✓ God gave the Israelites a law which said one-tenth of all they had should be set apart as holy and given to God (Leviticus 27:30,32).
✓ Tithing is a way to obey God's commands and honor Him with your possessions.
✓ Tithing reminds you that everything you have comes from God.

PRAY Ask God to help you understand the importance of tithing. Ask Him to help you remember He gave you all that you have.

DAY 5

A PERSONAL ISSUE

VERSE OF THE DAY: Malachi 3:10 / CHALLENGE: Mark 12:41-44

DO! Write *My Tithe* on the front on an envelope. Count the amount of money you have in a bank or wallet. For each dollar you have, place one dime in the envelope. Take your tithe to church with you on Sunday and place the envelope in the offering plate.

Whenever you receive money as payment for something or as a gift, set aside one-tenth as an offering to God.

 KNOW!

✓ God loves you and wants to bless you.

✓ God promises if you are faithful to give Him your tithe, He will pour out so many blessings that you will not have room for them all!

✓ You do not have to tell people how much money you give (that is between you and God).

✓ A tithe is one-tenth, but you can give more than one-tenth.

PRAY Praise God for all of the things He gives you. Ask Him to help you be faithful with your tithe.

DAY 6

WHERE'S YOUR TREASURE?

VERSE OF THE DAY: Matthew 6:21 / CHALLENGE: Matthew 6:19-20

 DO!

Write each item in the correct place in the puzzle.

CARS
DOLLS
SHOES
BASEBALL CARDS
INSECTS
STAMPS
POSTCARDS
AUTOGRAPHS
TSHIRTS

These are all things some people collect. Do you collect anything? If so, what? _____. How valuable is your collection? Where will your collection be next year? In 10 years? In 20 years?

 KNOW!

✓ God wants you to keep your priorities in order. Collecting things is OK, but don't let them become the most important part of your life.

✓ God wants you to focus on your relationship with Him, and telling other people about Jesus.

✓ You may get rid of the things you collect, but your relationship with God is forever.

✓ You can use your time, talents, and possessions to help people learn about God and Jesus.

PRAY Thank God for your greatest treasure—Jesus.

HOW MY OFFERING HELPS

1. **DOWN**
Without my offerings, my church would not be able to have a
_____ to meet together for worship and Bible study.

2. **ACROSS**
Part of my offerings are used to pay our _____ for the
ministries they provide.

3. **DOWN**
The _____ is churches working together to provide ministries
such as the International Mission Board, North American Mission Board,
seminaries, colleges, and others that help people learn about Jesus.

4. **DOWN**
Materials and Bibles are bought for people of all ages to have
_____.

5. **DOWN**
My offerings help provide _____ for families who cannot
afford to buy it.

6. **ACROSS**
Without my offerings, our church would not have many of the
_____ we need such as paper, crayons, markers, and glue.

7. **DOWN**
Have you ever wondered how much the _____ such as lights
and heat cost? My offering helps pay for these things.

8. **ACROSS**
Part of my offering is used to help people
in my town, state, country, and
around the world learn how much
Jesus loves them. This is called
supporting _____.

WORD BANK

Bible Studies

Church Building

Church Staff

Cooperative Program

Food

Missions

Supplies

Utilities

HOW DO I STAND UP FOR WHAT I BELIEVE?

JON MERRYMAN

Now that you are a Christian, you want to confess (tell what you know) your faith in Jesus to as many people as possible! That is a very good thing! As you tell about Jesus, you may find people who:

◎ do not believe what you believe,
◎ do not want to hear your beliefs, and
◎ believe something different than you believe.

Knowing why you believe what you believe and how to share your beliefs is important. You may think *I believe these things because I heard them at church* or *my parents told me.* For some people, more proof is needed to know why they should believe the same things. God does not force people to believe the same things. He gives people the freedom to choose what they believe. As you read the Bible, you will discover how the prophets tried to help people know about God. You will also discover how Jesus, Peter, Paul, and many other people taught people about the one true God.

While people may try to tell you the Bible is not true, or God does not exist, you know the Bible and God as absolute truth. No one can dispute what God is doing in YOUR life. The things happening in your life are your story and how can anyone say your story is not true? Before you begin telling someone what she should believe, you need to know what you believe.

Do you believe these things?

◎ GOD—is the only one true God, who loved the world so much He gave His one and only Son to die for the sins of all people.
◎ JESUS—is God's one and only Son who lived a perfect, sinless life; willingly died on the cross for all people; was buried and God raised Him from the dead.
◎ BIBLE—is the true Word of God and has meaning for all people.
◎ SALVATION—is a free gift God gives people who ask Jesus to be their Savior and Lord; is not earned by being good or doing a lot of good works.

When someone says, "I don't go to church—I don't believe in God," you can say, "Can I tell you about what God has done in MY life?" While the person may not believe what you tell her, you've left her with a true story—God's story in YOU.

So do not be afraid—be bold! Here are some tips on standing up for what you believe:

◎ Know what you believe and why you believe it.
◎ Know where in the Bible to support the things you believe.
◎ Pray for the Holy Spirit to help you tell people what you believe.
◎ Do not argue with people who believe things differently than you.
◎ Do not force people to believe what you believe.
◎ Live out what you believe.

DAY 1 — AT HOME

VERSES OF THE DAY: Ephesians 6:1-3
CHALLENGE: Luke 2:41-52

 On the house below, write the names of people who live in your home.

During the day, ask each person to tell you one or two things he believes about God and why.

How does what your family members believe compare to what you believe?

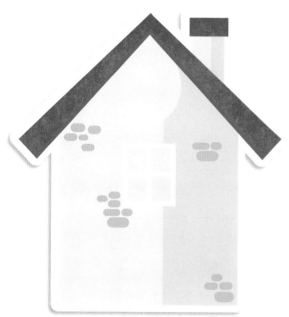

KNOW!

✓ Each person in your family deserves love and respect.
✓ God helps you know how to honor your parents and family members in everything—even sharing about Him.
✓ God wants your family to worship Him.

PRAY Thank God for your family. Pray for each person by name.

DAY 2 — AT SCHOOL

VERSES OF THE DAY: Ephesians 6:10-11
CHALLENGE: Ephesians 6:10-20

DO! Complete the dot to dot.

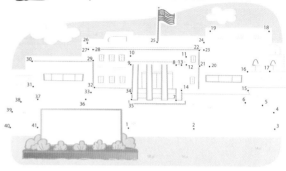

Write the name of your school on the sign.

How many of the people who you see every day at school are Christians?

How can you tell these people what you believe?

KNOW!

✓ God is always with you. He gave you the Holy Spirit to help you tell people about Jesus.
✓ The Devil (Satan) does not want you to tell people about Jesus.
✓ All Christians (yes, that's you, too) are called to tell people about Jesus.
✓ How you treat people can tell them what you believe about God.
✓ Do not force someone to listen to you tell about Jesus. You can cause a person never to want to hear about Jesus if she is not ready.
✓ Praying before tests, meals, and at other times during the day is a great way to tell about what you believe.

PRAY Pray for people at your school. Ask God to help you have the courage to tell what you believe.

HOW DO I STAND UP FOR WHAT I BELIEVE?   **81**

THROUGH YOUR WORDS

VERSE OF THE DAY: Ephesians 4:29 / CHALLENGE: Ephesians 4:17-29

DO! Think about the things you say every day. Are all of your words positive? Do you ever say something mean or untrue?

Write 5 positive and 5 negative words on the chart.

POSITIVE	NEGATIVE

Try to use more positive words today than negative ones.

KNOW!

✓ You can honor God with your words.
✓ Your words can lead others to follow God or turn away from Him.
✓ Your words show people the change God has made in your life.

PRAY Ask God to help you choose words that honor Him.

DAY 4

THROUGH YOUR ACTIONS

VERSE OF THE DAY: Proverbs 20:11 / CHALLENGE: Luke 10:25-37

DO! Color in the words that are not positive actions.

Argues	Listens	Lies
Respects	Protects	Encourages
Ignores	Helps	Makes fun of
Hits	Supports	Disobeys

What shape did you discover?

Think about how your actions tell people what you believe about God.

How does God want you to treat people? Do people want to listen to you tell about obeying God if you do not obey your parents or teachers? How can people know about God if you do not tell them?

KNOW!

✓ Your actions speak louder than your words. People see what you believe by the way you act.
✓ You can respond in positive ways to people who disagree or dislike you.
✓ Even when it is difficult to love people, you can love them because God loves them.

PRAY Ask God to help your actions tell what you believe about Him.

DAY 5

HAVE A DESIRE TO TELL

VERSE OF THE DAY: Psalm 66:16
CHALLENGE: Acts 21:27–22:29

DO! What is the best thing that has happened to you recently? Create a newspaper headline telling about the event.

Did you want people to know what happened to you? How did people respond?

✓ God wants you to tell people what you believe about Him.

✓ The Bible says for Christians to tell what they know about God and how people can accept Jesus as Savior and Lord.

✓ Jesus Himself told His followers to go to all parts of the world and tell about Him (Matthew 28:19-20; Acts 1:8).

✓ God places people in your life who need to hear about Jesus.

PRAY Pray that God will give you an excitement and desire to share about Him every day!

DAY 6

TELL THE WORLD

VERSE OF THE DAY: Acts 1:8
CHALLENGE: Acts 14

DO! If you could go anywhere in the world, where would you go? Draw a picture of yourself at the location.

✓ God created every person. He loves everyone and wants everyone to accept Jesus as his Savior and Lord.

✓ God wants everyone to help tell people around the world about Him.

✓ Missionaries are people chosen by God to tell another group of people the good news about Jesus.

✓ Many people in the world believe in different gods. Some people do not believe there is a God.

PRAY Pray for people around the world to believe in the one true God.

TESTIMONIES OF PEOPLE WHO STOOD UP FOR WHAT THEY BELIEVED

My name is Rosa Parks. I was born on Valentine's Day (February 14), 1913, in Alabama. I took my stand on December 1, 1955. I had worked hard all day and was tired and ready to go home. At this time, there were two sections on the city buses. People with black skin, like myself, were not allowed to sit in the section for white-skinned people. I took a seat in the white section and refused to stand up and give my seat to a white-skinned man. Because of my decision to stand up for what I believed, I was arrested and sent to jail.

Following my release from jail, African Americans began to stop riding the bus. A young man named Martin Luther King, Jr., led a boycott against the bus system. The boycott lasted over a year. As a result, the bus companies had to close down because not enough people were riding the buses.

- ☺ What decisions did Rosa Parks make?
- ☺ How did her decision impact her life?
- ☺ How did her decision impact people around her?
- ☺ What would you have done if you were Rosa Parks?

My name is Eric Liddell. I was born in 1902 to missionaries serving in China. I really liked to play rugby and other sports. I ran a lot of races for my college, but did not have a lot of time for both running and rugby. I decided to focus on running, and in turn was chosen to run the 100-meter race in Paris in the 1924 Olympics. When I discovered the race was on Sunday, I decided not to run and changed to the 400-meter competition. I made my decision not to run on Sunday because of my commitment to God. I knew He wanted Sunday to be a day of rest, and I would not allow anything to change my mind. I won a gold medal in the 400-meter race and a bronze medal for the 200-meter race.

When the Olympics were over, I returned to China and served as a missionary from 1925 to 1943. In 1941, life in China became very dangerous. The British Government told all the British citizens to leave China. My wife and children left for Canada, but I stayed. I was forced to live in a Japanese war camp from 1943 until my death in 1945.

- ☺ What decisions did Eric Liddell make?
- ☺ How did his decisions impact his life?
- ☺ How did his decisions impact people around him?
- ☺ What would you have done if you were Eric Liddell?

TESTIMONIES OF PEOPLE WHO STOOD UP FOR WHAT THEY BELIEVED

My name is Martin Luther. I helped translate the Bible into the German language, but that is not all I did. At the age of 17, I began my college education. In just one year, I received my college degree. Three years later, I had my Master's degree. My father wanted me to become a lawyer so I started law school. That all changed when, during a thunderstorm, a lightening bolt nearly struck me. I was so scared I said I would become a monk (a man who withdraws from the world for religious reasons). I dropped out of law school and began living as a monk.

I tried to follow all the religious duties of a monk, however, I did not feel close to God. One of my religious leaders said I needed more schooling. Following more studying, I began teaching. My study of the Bible helped me better understand things about God. I believed what the church was doing at the time was not what the Bible taught. I felt that God's gift of salvation was received by faith, and trust in God's promise to forgive sins because of Jesus' death on the cross. On October 31, 1517, I nailed my "95 Theses" to a church door. I said the Roman Catholic church was not correctly teaching what the Bible said. The things I wrote were not accepted by many people. I was told to say what I had written was wrong. I said that I was sorry for how I had stated many things, but I agreed with what I wrote. Since I would not say what I wrote was wrong, I was declared an outlaw.

A friend of mine helped me escape from harm. He arranged for me to be captured by a masked horseman. I lived for a year in a castle in Wartburg, Germany. During the time, I worked on translating the Bible into the German language. The Luther German New Testament translation was published for the first time in 1522. The Old Testament was not completed until 1534.

- ☺ What decisions did Martin Luther make?
- ☺ How did his decisions impact his life?
- ☺ How did his decisions impact people around him?
- ☺ What would you have done if you were Martin Luther?

WHAT ABOUT PEOPLE WHO BELIEVE DIFFERENT THINGS?

JON MERRYMAN

The next time you are at the grocery store, library, school, or park, look around at the people. Do all the people look the same? Do they all wear the same types of clothing? Do they all eat the same types of food? God created people unique. Just as people are unique in the way they look, dress, and eat, they are different in what they believe. While you can hope everyone believes that Jesus is God's Son who died on the cross for the forgiveness of sin and was raised from the dead, not everyone believes these true facts.

Here are some things other people believe (more are found on pages 90-91):

- Jehovah's Witnesses believe you must earn your salvation.
- Mormons believe men who live a good life can become gods.
- New Age followers believe everything and everyone is a god.
- Islam teaches Jesus is not the Son of God, nor was He crucified.
- Hindus believe Jesus' death does not provide forgiveness of sin.
- Buddhists believe there is no god.

How do you think God feels about these beliefs? How does it make you feel to know people believe different things that are not true?

Here are some tips to help you know how to share what you believe with people who believe different things:

- Know what you believe—why do you believe in the one true God?
- Know where in the Bible you can find verses to support what you believe.
- Realize not everyone will believe the same things as you.
- Do not argue with people over what they believe. You can disagree with what the people believe, but be a positive example to people.
- Pray for people who believe different things about God.
- Remember, God loves all people and wants them to accept Jesus as Savior and Lord.

How did you come to know Jesus as your Savior and Lord? More than likely, you heard about Jesus at church, from a friend, family member, or teacher. Once you learned the truth about God, you prayed and asked Jesus to come into your life to be your Savior and Lord. Remember, kids who believe different things may have not heard about the one true God that you know—and He might use you to tell them!

DAY 1 — TRUST THE BIBLE

VERSE OF THE DAY: John 8:32 / CHALLENGE: Acts 17:1-10

DO! Place a check mark beside the statements you know to be true:

☐ 2+2=4

☐ THE EARTH IS ROUND.

☐ SQUIRRELS ARE ANIMALS.

☐ YOU CANNOT LIVE WITHOUT BREATHING.

☐ JESUS IS GOD'S ONE AND ONLY SON.

How did you know these things to be true? If someone told you 2+2=5, how would you know she is wrong?

KNOW!

✓ Bible truths never change.
✓ God inspired (told) real people to write the Bible.
✓ You can be confident (sure) that God is real by the evidence of His work in your life and in the lives of others you know.
✓ The Bible has truth and meaning for all people.

PRAY Pray God will give you confidence and opportunities to share what you believe with people who have different beliefs.

DAY 2 — KNOW THE BIBLE

VERSE OF THE DAY: Acts 17:11 / CHALLENGE: Acts 17:10-15

DO! Place a check mark beside the facts that are in the Bible.

☐ BABY RESCUED FROM FLOATING BASKET

☐ DISCIPLE BETRAYS JESUS

☐ GIANT KILLED BY BOY WITH SLINGSHOT

☐ JESUS DEAD! NOW ALIVE!

☐ LIONS DO NOT EAT MAN

Did you check all of them? Each of these facts is in the Bible. Knowing and understanding how to find information in the Bible is important. When someone asks you why you believe something, you need to be able to locate proof in the Bible.

KNOW!

✓ The Bible says there is one true God (Jeremiah 10:10).
✓ The Bible says Jesus is the only way to eternal life (John 14:6).
✓ The Bible says Jesus will return to earth (John 14:1-4).
✓ The Bible says all people have sinned (Romans 3:23).
✓ The Bible teaches being good and working hard will not earn you a place in heaven (Ephesians 2:8-9).

PRAY Ask God to help you learn what the Bible teaches and how to use the information to tell about your faith.

DAY 3 — ACCEPT AND RESPECT OTHERS

VERSE OF THE DAY: 1 Peter 3:16
CHALLENGE: Acts 17:22-34

 Write how you would respond to this situation.

Rather than attacking someone for what she believes, show God's love to her.

KNOW!

✓ God respects all people, even if they do not believe in Him.
✓ God holds you accountable for the way you treat people.
✓ God does not hold you accountable for what other people believe, but He does hold you accountable for what you tell people.

PRAY Ask God to help you love and encourage people who believe different things.

DAY 4 — SPEAK THE TRUTH

VERSES OF THE DAY: Galatians 1:6-7
CHALLENGE: John 3:1-18

 Read the list of things some other people believe (page 90).

How does it make you feel to know people believe these things?

_____

_____

_____

Are you concerned that these people do not know the one true God?

_____

Compare the list of things Christians believe (page 91) to what other faiths believe (page 90).

KNOW!

✓ God holds each person accountable for what he believes.
✓ God wants Christians to tell the truth about what the Bible teaches and what people should believe.
✓ You can tell people what you believe about God.
✓ You need to know what you believe and how to support your beliefs so when you hear things that are not correct, you can speak up.

PRAY Pray for courage to speak the truth to people.

DAY 5

PRAY FOR PEOPLE WHO BELIEVE DIFFERENT THINGS

VERSE OF THE DAY: 1 Timothy 2:1 / CHALLENGE: James 5:13-20

DO! In the spaces, write the names of three people you know.

Person's Name	How God Answered Prayer

Ask the people, "Has God ever answered your prayers? If so, how?" Write the people's responses in the space beside the names.

Think about your prayers. In what ways has God answered your prayers?

✓ Prayer is a great way to help people who believe different things about God.
✓ You can pray for people even when they will not listen to what you believe.
✓ God hears and answers prayers.

PRAY Pray for people who believe things that are not true. Ask God to help the people know what they believe is wrong and to know the truth.

DAY 6

GOD CAN CHANGE LIVES THROUGH YOU

VERSE OF THE DAY: Isaiah 6:8 / CHALLENGE: Acts 9:1-20

DO! Complete the pictures of you as a baby and now.

In what ways have you changed? Do you like the same foods? What can you do now that you could not do as a baby?

Think about your life since becoming a Christian. How are you different now than the day you accepted Jesus as your Savior and Lord? Do you know things that you did not know then? Do you pray more? Are you more concerned about telling people about Jesus?

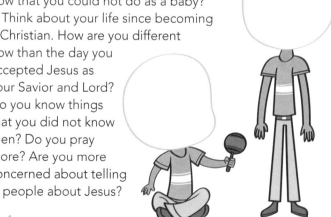

✓ When you accepted Jesus Christ as your Savior and Lord, your life changed. You will never be the same again.
✓ God can use you to help change people's lives. You can tell people the truth.
✓ God wants you to be willing to be used by Him.

PRAY Thank God for using you to help people know the truth about Him.

WHAT SOME PEOPLE BELIEVE

Here are some things different religious groups believe.

GOD

→ Mormons believe God was once a man, but over time became a god.
→ Jehovah's Witnesses believe God is called Jehovah and that He is not Father, Son, and Holy Spirit.
→ Hindus believe everyone is part of God.

JESUS

→ Jehovah's Witnesses do not believe Jesus is God. They believe Jesus died on a stake, not a cross. Jesus is not coming again.
→ Mormons believe Jesus was married. His death does not provide for the forgiveness of sin.
→ New Age followers do not believe Jesus is God's Son, nor is He a Savior.

SALVATION

→ Jehovah's Witnesses believe you must be baptized as a Jehovah's Witness and that you must earn your salvation by works.
→ Mormons believe a person is saved through good works. You cannot have eternal life if you are not a Mormon.
→ Christian Science followers do not believe death is real.
→ Buddhists believe the goal of life is to be released to nirvana (freedom from the endless cycle of personal reincarnation).

HOLY SPIRIT

→ Jehovah's Witnesses do not believe in the Holy Spirit as a part of the Father, Son, and Holy Spirit.
→ Mormons believe the Holy Spirit is not God.
→ Islam rejects the idea of the Trinity (Father, Son, and Holy Spirit).
→ Buddhists do not believe in spirits, therefore they do not believe in the Holy Spirit.

AFTERLIFE ON EARTH

→ Jehovah's Witnesses believe 144,000 people will become spirits in heaven. The rest of the believers will remain on earth and must live perfect lives for 1,000 years.
→ Mormons believe people go to one of three heavens, some people even become gods.
→ Buddhists believe people are reincarnated (continue to come back to life until they live good enough lives to be released from this world).

WHAT CHRISTIANS BELIEVE

GOD

God is the one true God.

God created the world from nothing.

God loves and values all people.

God is worthy of praise and worship.

God is almighty, all-powerful, all-knowing, and always present.

God is all-eternal, holy, and perfect.

JESUS

Jesus came to earth in human form.

Jesus is the one and only Son of God.

Jesus died to pay the penalty for sin.

Jesus died on a cross and God raised Him from the dead.

Jesus will return to earth.

Jesus lived a perfect life.

HOLY SPIRIT

The Holy Spirit is part of the Trinity (Father, Son, and the Holy Spirit).

The Holy Spirit helps people know, understand, and remember all things about God.

The Holy Spirit inspired Bible writers to know what to write.

The Holy Spirit helps believers tell people about Jesus.

The Holy Spirit helps believers grow as Christians.

SALVATION

Salvation is a free gift from God.

Without a Savior, the punishment for sin is eternal death and hell.

When the Holy Spirit convicts people of sin, they can trust Jesus as their personal Savior and Lord.

After physical death on earth, Christians will spend eternity with God in heaven.

HOW DO I TELL MY FRIENDS ABOUT JESUS?

CINDY LEACH

What happens when you hear exciting news or something great happens to you? Do you keep the news all to yourself? No—you tell about it! You tell so everyone knows the amazing thing that's happened.

The truth about Jesus is exciting, fantastic, and amazing news! In fact, the word *gospel* means "good news." Good news is meant to be shared!

Here are some reasons why it's important for you to tell your friends about Jesus and the great thing that has happened to you.

- God wants you to be involved in His work. God uses people to accomplish His plan. He wants every person to know about Jesus. As Christians tell other people about Jesus, the gospel (good news) spreads. In Romans 10:14, the Bible asks, "How can people believe if they have not heard about Jesus, and how can they hear unless people are willing to tell?" Your friends cannot choose to believe the good news of Jesus until they hear about it. Are you willing to tell them?
- God wants you to follow the example and teachings of Jesus. Jesus spent His time on earth telling people the truth about God and encouraging them to live God's way. Jesus told His disciples to go to all parts of the world and tell everyone about God (Mark 16:15). You can follow Jesus' example and obey His teachings when you tell your friends the good news of Jesus.
- God wants you to tell people about Jesus and what He has done for them—and for YOU! When you became a Christian, you chose to accept God's assignment for you. That assignment includes telling your friends the truth about God and how Jesus changed your life and can change their lives, too.

So who can you tell? Begin by telling the people closest to you—your family and friends. Next, tell people on your soccer team or those you see every day at school or in your neighborhood. Then tell people who you do not know very well. God wants everyone to hear the good news about Jesus.

Now you know WHY you need to tell your friends about Jesus. You know WHO you can tell about Jesus. Now discover HOW you can tell your friends about Jesus. As you study this week, you will discover that telling your friends about Jesus is easier than you think. You have good news to share. Start spreading the gospel!

DAY 1
ACCEPT THE RESPONSIBILITY

VERSES OF THE DAY: MATTHEW 28:19-20
CHALLENGE: ACTS 8:26-39

 List the names of six friends. Check whether your friends are Christians or not.

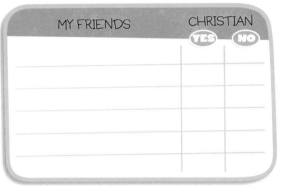

MY FRIENDS	CHRISTIAN	
	YES	NO

How do you know if your friends are Christians?

KNOW!

✓ Many people may act like Christians, but actions do not make a person a Christian. Some people may go to church, but going to church does not make a person a Christian. Only accepting Jesus as Savior and Lord makes a person a Christian.

✓ When you talk with a friend about Jesus, here are some important things to share.
  ✱ Everyone sins. (Romans 3:23)
  ✱ Sin separates you from God but He offers forgiveness from sin. (Romans 6:23)
  ✱ God loves you and sent Jesus to die on the cross to pay for your sin. (Romans 5:8)
  ✱ You can ADMIT you are a sinner, BELIEVE that Jesus is God's Son and accept God's forgiveness from sin, and CONFESS your faith in Jesus Christ as Savior and Lord (Romans 10:9-10,13).

PRAY Ask God to help you tell your friends about Jesus.

DAY 2
CHECK YOUR SPEECH

VERSE OF THE DAY: PSALM 34:13
CHALLENGE: JAMES 1:19-27

 Read aloud the following sentence.

"MAY I PLEASE HAVE AN APPLE?"

Now read the sentence using these different tones of voice:

☐ angry   ☐ sleepy
☐ sweet   ☐ cranky
☐ whiny   ☐ bossy

Which tones of voice would most likely get someone to give you an apple?

When you tell your friends about Jesus, it's not only WHAT you say, but HOW you say it that is important.

KNOW!

✓ Your actions, not just your words, should tell others what you believe about Jesus.

✓ God loves everyone and wants you to tell your friends about Jesus with kindness and compassion.

✓ When you act like Jesus did, your friends will be more likely to listen when you tell them about Jesus.

✓ Followers of Jesus will want to become more like Him. Jesus' actions always helped people know about God.

PRAY Ask God to help your words and actions match what you believe about Him.

DAY 3

BE PREPARED TO TELL YOUR STORY

VERSES OF THE DAY: Acts 4:18-20 / CHALLENGE: Acts 26:1-23

DO! Complete page 97.

Before becoming a Christian, I _____

_____

I became a Christian when I _____

_____

Now my life is different because _____

_____

_____

Stand in front of a mirror and practice telling the story of how you became a Christian. Pretend you are talking to a friend. You can use what you wrote above to get started.

✓ God wants you to tell your friends about Jesus.
✓ You have a unique story about becoming a Christian.
✓ You can tell a friend about Jesus by sharing what He has done for you.

PRAY Say: "Thank You, God, for giving me a story to tell because of Jesus. Help me always be prepared to tell people what You did for me."

DAY 4

KNOW HOW TO USE THE BIBLE

VERSE OF THE DAY: 2 Timothy 2:15 / CHALLENGE: 2 Timothy 3:14-17

DO! Find and mark the following verses in your Bible.
☐ Romans 3:23   ☐ Romans 6:23
☐ I John 1:9   ☐ Acts 3:19
☐ John 3:16   ☐ Ephesians 2:8-9
☐ Romans 10:13

Close your Bible and practice locating the verses.
    Choose one of the verses. With your parents' permission, use a dry erase marker and write the verse on your bathroom mirror. Try to memorize the verse.
    Do the same thing with other verses.

✓ God's Word (the Bible) explains what Jesus did and how a person can become a Christian.
✓ The more you learn about God's Word, the better prepared you will be to talk with your friends about Jesus.
✓ The more you practice locating Bible verses in your Bible, the easier it will become.

PRAY Ask God to help you know how to use the Bible when you tell your friends about Jesus.

DAY 5

TRUST GOD'S POWER

VERSE OF THE DAY: Luke 1:37
CHALLENGE: Acts 10:34-48

 Use your Bible to match each statement to the correct passage.

Giant Killed with Slingshot ∘   ∘ Exodus 14:15-29

Peter Set Free through Prayer ∘   ∘ 1 Samuel 17

Crossed on Dry Land ∘   ∘ Luke 24:1-12

Jesus Raised from the Dead ∘   ∘ Acts 12:6-7

What do these Bible stories tell you about God's power? Do you think if God has the power to do these things He has the power to help you tell your friends about Jesus?

✓ You can depend on God's power to help you tell your friends about Jesus.
✓ The Holy Spirit helps Christians tell what they know about Jesus.
✓ God loves people of all nationalities and cultures. He wants everyone to hear about Jesus. This includes your friends.
✓ You may be scared to tell about Jesus, but God will give you the words and courage.

PRAY Thank God for His power that helps you tell your friends about Jesus.

DAY 6

BE PATIENT, LET GOD BE IN CONTROL

VERSE OF THE DAY: 2 Peter 3:9
CHALLENGE: Acts 26:24-31

 Do you like to wait? Why?
Locate a watch that counts seconds.
Start the watch and sit still for 60 seconds.

Was it difficult to sit still? Why?

✓ God is patient. He wants everyone to know Him and choose to follow Jesus.
✓ God gives all people a choice. Some people choose to say "yes" to God, others say "no."
✓ Your responsibility is to tell everyone the truth about Jesus, but do not pressure people to accept Jesus as Savior and Lord.
✓ The Holy Spirit will help people know when it is time for them to become Christians.
✓ Each person is accountable to God for the decisions he makes.
✓ God loves all people and wants them to accept Jesus as Savior and Lord, but He will not force anyone to do so.

PRAY Thank God that He has the power to do all things. Pray for patience as you tell people about Jesus.

ABCs OF BECOMING A CHRISTIAN

Becoming a Christian is the most important decision
anyone can ever make.

WHAT DOES THE BIBLE SAY ABOUT BECOMING A CHRISTIAN?

✓ God loves you. (John 3:16)
✓ Sin is choosing your way instead of God's way. Sin separates people from God. (Romans 3:23)
✓ God sent Jesus so you would not have to die for your sin. Jesus died on the cross, He was buried, and God raised Him from the dead. (Romans 5:8)

HOW TO BECOME A CHRISTIAN

ADMIT to God you are a sinner. (Romans 2:23) Repent, turn away from your sin. (Acts 3:19; 1 John 1:9)

BELIEVE that Jesus is God's Son and accept God's gift of forgiveness from sin. (Acts 16:31; Acts 4:12; John 14:6; Ephesians 2:8-9)

CONFESS your faith in Jesus Christ as Savior and Lord. (Romans 10:9-10,13)

The Holy Spirit will help a person know when it is time to become a Christian.
If it is not time for your friend to become a Christian,
do not push her to do so. God will help her know the right time. If your friend
wants to become a Christian, you can help her pray a prayer like this:

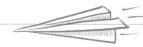

I know I have sinned and my sin separates me from You. I am sorry for my sin. I believe Jesus died on the cross for me so my sin can be forgiven. I believe Jesus rose from the dead and is alive. God, please forgive me. I ask Jesus to come into my life and be my Savior and Lord. I will obey You and live for You the rest of my life. Thank You. In Jesus' name I pray, Amen.

TESTIMONY PAGE

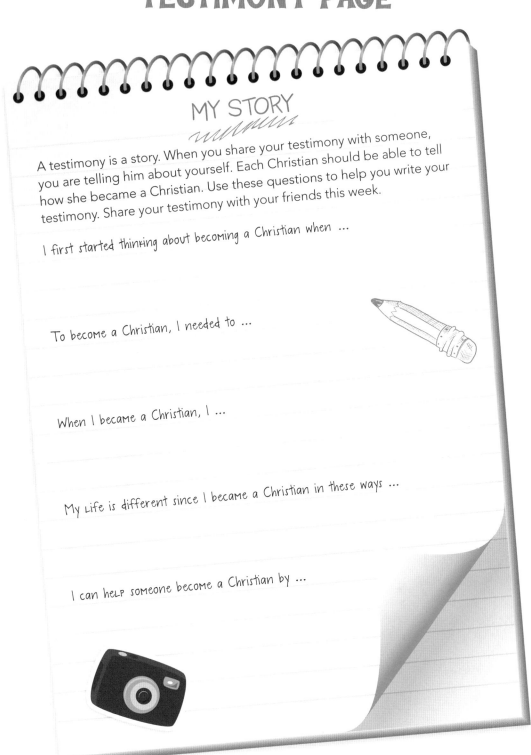

MY STORY

A testimony is a story. When you share your testimony with someone, you are telling him about yourself. Each Christian should be able to tell how she became a Christian. Use these questions to help you write your testimony. Share your testimony with your friends this week.

I first started thinking about becoming a Christian when ...

To become a Christian, I needed to ...

When I became a Christian, I ...

My Life is different since I became a Christian in these ways ...

I can help someone become a Christian by ...

THE BOOKS OF THE NEW TESTAMENT

The New Testament has 27 different books.
The books are separated into 5 divisions.

GOSPELS

MATTHEW (MATH <u>yoo</u>) was originally written for the Jews and shows Jesus as the Messiah and King.

JOHN (JAHN) emphasizes Jesus is the Son of God and that by believing in Him, people can have eternal life.

LUKE (L<u>OO</u>K [LEWK]) was written for the Greeks. Luke wrote about Jesus' humanity and His death on the cross.

MARK (MAHRK) was written for the Gentiles (non-Jews), and presents Jesus as the Son of Man.

NEW TESTAMENT HISTORY

ACTS (AKTS) tells what the apostles did during the time after Jesus' crucifixion, resurrection, and return to heaven. Luke wrote this book and reported the coming of the Holy Spirit and the growth of the church.

PAUL'S LETTERS

1 AND 2 CORINTHIANS (koh RIN thih uhns) were written to the Christians at Corinth in Greece. Paul wrote about sin in the church at Corinth and stressed church unity. Paul defended his own authority and spoke against the false teachers in Corinth.

GALATIANS (guh LAY shuhnz) was written to the Christians in the province of Galatia, in Asia Minor. The theme is the freedom of the gospel as opposed to the bondage of the law.

PHILIPPIANS (fih LIP ih uhnz) written to the church in Philippi, thanked the believers for their kindness toward Paul and explained true joy in Christ.

ROMANS (ROH muhnz) was written to Christians in Rome and is about living in ways that please God because of faith in Him.

EPHESIANS (ih FEE shuhnz) was written to teach Christians they have been saved by grace and should live like God wants them to live so that they can stand against the ways of Satan.

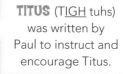

TITUS (TIGH tuhs) was written by Paul to instruct and encourage Titus.

1 AND 2 TIMOTHY (TIM uh thih) are letters of encouragement and wisdom that Paul wrote to his young helper Timothy. The first letter is about church leadership. The second letter gave final instructions and encouragement to Timothy.

PHILEMON (figh LEE muhn) was written by Paul to encourage Philemon to forgive his runaway slave Onesimus and treat him as a brother in Christ.

1 AND 2 THESSALONIANS (THESS uh LOH nih hnz) addressed the church in Thessalonica in Greece. In the first letter, Paul praised the church's faithfulness and helped them understand more about Christ's return. The second letter told about events that will happen before Jesus' return and stressed patience.

1, 2, AND 3 JOHN (JAHN) were written by the same man who wrote the Gospel of John. In the first letter, he reminded Christians of God's love, encouraged them to love one another, and warned them about false teaching. The second letter has messages about love and truth and also warned about false teaching. In the third letter, John thanked a man named Gaius for his kindness toward missionaries.

GENERAL LETTERS

JAMES (JAYMZ) was written by Jesus' brother and tells that true faith is shown in right behavior.

COLOSSIANS (kuh LAHSH uhnz) encouraged the church in Colossae to obey Jesus' teachings and warned the people to stay away from teachings that are not true.

HEBREWS (HEE brooz) explains why Jesus came to earth to be the Savior of the world and encouraged Jewish Christians by helping them understand how Jesus fulfilled their law.

1 AND 2 PETER (PE tuhr) were written by Peter. In the first letter, he encouraged Christians to be patient under persecution. In the second letter, he encouraged them to be holy and to be careful about false teachers.

JUDE (JOOD) written by Jesus' and James' brother, encouraged all Christians to stand firm in the faith.

NEW TESTAMENT PROPHECY

REVELATION (REV uh LAY shuhn) was written by John. He encouraged and warned Christians about events leading to the end of time and the coming of "a new heaven and a new earth."

MY SERMON NOTES

TODAY'S DATE

TODAY'S SCRIPTURE
READING/SERMON

THINGS MY PASTOR SAID:

SOMETHING I LEARNED TODAY:

SOMETHING I CAN DO THIS WEEK RELATED TO THE SERMON:

SOMETHING I CAN TALK WITH MY FAMILY ABOUT:

MY SERMON NOTES

TODAY'S DATE

TODAY'S SCRIPTURE READING/SERMON

THINGS MY PASTOR SAID:

SOMETHING I LEARNED TODAY:

SOMETHING I CAN DO THIS WEEK RELATED TO THE SERMON:

SOMETHING I CAN TALK WITH MY FAMILY ABOUT:

MY SERMON NOTES

TODAY'S DATE

TODAY'S SCRIPTURE
READING/SERMON

THINGS MY PASTOR SAID:

SOMETHING I LEARNED TODAY:

SOMETHING I CAN DO THIS WEEK RELATED TO THE SERMON:

SOMETHING I CAN TALK WITH MY FAMILY ABOUT:

MY SERMON NOTES

TODAY'S DATE

TODAY'S SCRIPTURE
READING/SERMON

THINGS MY PASTOR SAID:

SOMETHING I LEARNED TODAY:

SOMETHING I CAN DO THIS WEEK RELATED TO THE SERMON:

SOMETHING I CAN TALK WITH MY FAMILY ABOUT:

MY SERMON NOTES

THINGS MY PASTOR SAID:

TODAY'S DATE

TODAY'S SCRIPTURE
READING/SERMON

SOMETHING I LEARNED TODAY:

SOMETHING I CAN DO THIS WEEK RELATED TO THE SERMON:

SOMETHING I CAN TALK WITH MY FAMILY ABOUT:

MY SERMON NOTES

THINGS MY PASTOR SAID:

SOMETHING I LEARNED TODAY:

SOMETHING I CAN DO THIS WEEK RELATED TO THE SERMON:

SOMETHING I CAN TALK WITH MY FAMILY ABOUT:

WHAT COMES NEXT?

How Do I Keep Growing in My Relationship With God?

Congratulations! You completed your I'm a Christian, Now What? journal. Think about some of the things you learned. In what ways have you grown closer to God as you studied the Bible, completed the activities, and prayed?

Do you want to keep growing in your relationship with God? God wants you to.

Here are some suggestions to how you can keep growing:

☐ Attend Bible study classes at your church.

☐ Participate in worship services.

☐ Read and study your Bible daily.

☐ Pray.

☐ Memorize Bible verses.

☐ Tell your friends what you know about God.

☐ Ask questions when you do not understand things.

☐ Talk with people who you know have a close relationship with God.

☐ Read stories of people who had close relationships with God.

☐ Be open to God doing amazing things in your life.

PARENT/CHILD FOLLOW-UP COMMITMENT

Your child has completed the *I'm a Christian, Now What?* journal. Take time to celebrate with your child. Please do not see the completion of the journal as a final step in growing closer to God. The journey continues. Here are a few suggestions to help your child continue growing in his relationship with God:

✓ Participate as a family in corporate worship services.
✓ Ensure your child participates regularly in Bible study times.
✓ Set an example for your child as you grow in your relationship with God.

✓ Model Christ-like characteristics.
✓ Pray for and with your family on a daily basis.
✓ Look for opportunities to minister and serve in your community and around the world.
✓ Accept your God-given responsibility to nurture your child.
✓ Provide additional resources for your child to grow in his spiritual life.
✓ Ensure what your child learns is true biblical teaching.

You and your child began this journal by making a pledge to one another. End this journal in the same format.

PARENT'S PLEDGE

☐ I promise to continue praying for and encouraging you each day.
☐ I promise to live my life in a way that will provide a positive example for you to learn from.
☐ I promise to help you grow in your spiritual life by participating in regular worship times as a family and with our church family.
☐ I promise to allow God to work in your life as He sees best (not as I see best).
☐ I promise to support and encourage you as you grow in your relationship with God.

_____   _____
Parent's Signature   Date

CHILD'S PLEDGE

☐ I promise to continue growing in my relationship with God.
☐ I promise to seek to obey you and follow God's plan for our family.
☐ I promise to pray each day.
☐ I promise to allow God to work in my life as He sees best.
☐ I promise to talk with you and ask questions about my relationship with God.

_____   _____
Child's Signature   Date

MEET THE WRITERS

All of us writers for *I'm a Christian, Now What?* have a common goal—to help you grow in your relationship with God. We pray the things we wrote will help you learn how much God loves you and how you can tell people how they can accept Jesus as Savior and Lord. Because you are a Christian, we all have a common relationship— we are all part of God's family. Thanks for letting us help you grow as a Christian.

TODD CAPPS teaches children at Tulip Grove Baptist Church in Hermitage, TN. He is married to Kim and has two children, Paige and Carrington. When Mr. Todd is not working, he enjoys watching football, playing games, and reading.

ALISON CREEL and her husband, Adam, live in Murfreesboro, TN with their three daughters: Audrey, Anna, and Adeline. Mrs. Alison teaches third graders at Northside Baptist Church and serves as the Vacation Bible School director. Mrs. Alison likes writing, cake decorating, and teaching piano.

BILL EMEOTT teaches children at First Baptist Church, Nashville, TN. Mr. Bill works at LifeWay Christian Resources and gets to help children's Sunday School teachers, parents, and other church leaders know how to teach children.

RANDY FIELDS is the senior pastor at New Covenant Baptist Church in Grass Valley, CA. He is married to Robin and has two boys, Cameron and Austin. Pastor Randy enjoys spending time with family, hiking, and being on the lake.

AMY GRUBB teaches children at Faith Christian Academy in Waynesboro, Georgia. She is married to Robert and has three children, Adam, Mary, and David. Mrs. Amy loves playing outdoors with her kids and reading a good book after the kids go to bed.

VICKI HULSEY teaches children at Hermitage Hills Baptist Church in Hermitage, TN. She also has a Backyard Kids' Club at her home where boys and girls come to learn about Jesus, sing songs, play games, make crafts, and have yummy snacks. When Miss Vicki is not working, she enjoys music, reading, making cards, and having fun with the kids in her neighborhood.

CINDY LEACH is the Minister to Children at North Richland Hills Baptist Church in North Richland Hills, Texas. She and her husband Jason have two teenage daughters, Melissa and Carrie. Mrs. Cindy has lived in Texas all her life, but has never owned a pair of cowboy boots.

JON MERRYMAN teaches preteens at Second Baptist Church in Arkadelphia, AR. He loves to travel, write, and speak to kids and students around the country. Jon and his wife Emily work at Ouachita Baptist University and have one son, Dennis, whom they adopted from Moldova in 2008.

JERRY VOGEL is married to Janie and has four children, twelve grandchildren, and one granddog. Jerry teaches children at Brentwood Baptist Church in Brentwood, TN. Jerry and his wife enjoy traveling.

Check out these devotional magazines at **WWW.LIFEWAY.COM/KIDS.**

More

Adventure

BIBLE EXPRESS™

WANT TO LEARN MORE WORDS ABOUT THE BIBLE? CHECK OUT THIS GREAT BIBLE DICTIONARY.

Holman Bible Dictionary for Kids (00526845)

FOR ORDERING INFORMATION, CONTACT A LIFEWAY CUSTOMER SERVICE REPRESENTATIVE (1-800-458-2772).

THIS CERTIFICATE IS AWARDED TO

_____

ON _____
(Date)

FOR COMPLETING THE

I'M A CHRISTIAN, NOW WHAT? JOURNAL

_____
(Parent's Signature)